GREAT MOVIE HEROES

D1528044

*the text of this book is printed
on 100% recycled paper*

GREAT MOVIE HEROES

James Robert Parish

HARPER & ROW, PUBLISHERS
NEW YORK, EVANSTON, SAN FRANCISCO, LONDON

ACKNOWLEDGMENTS

Research Associate: Gregory Mank
Editor: T. Allan Taylor

✿　✿　✿　✿

Richard Braff, Bruco Enterprises, John Robert Cocchi, Morris Everett, Jr., Richard Hudson, Ken D. Jones, Kier's Photos, Doug McClelland, Albert B. Manski, Jim Meyer, Peter Miglierini, Movie Poster Service (Bob Smith), Movie Star News, Michael R. Pitts, Screen Facts (Alan G. Barbour), Charles Smith, Mrs. Peter Smith, and Florence Solomon.

Designed by Stephanie Krasnow.

First BARNES & NOBLE BOOKS edition published 1975

LIBRARY OF CONGRESS CATALOG CARD NUMBER: 75–549

STANDARD BOOK NUMBER: 06–465039–1

75 76 77 78 79 10 9 8 7 6 5 4 3 2 1

For Pippa White

Contents

CONTENTS

Preface

In the mid-1970s, the role of hero-worshiping in life has been greatly deemphasized. We are told that the general public no longer needs to transform certain figures into godlike beings. According to some trend observers, the average person these days prefers to focus on the common man and his workaday problems, joys, and aspirations.

The motion-picture industry, always anxious to keep pace with contemporary ideas, has accordingly presented few new candidates for superstar adulation. Gone for the most part are the bigger-than-life stars of the silver screen.

I found it nevertheless refreshing to reexamine the careers of a variety of cinema immortals. Each of the twenty-two performers studied here has contributed more than his share of vicarious pleasure for decades of moviegoers and TV late, late show viewers. Every one of these male stars has embellished his cinema work with an oversized, distinctive personality, memories of which linger on after the visual images of their pictures have faded from sight.

1. HUMPHREY BOGART

(HUMPHREY DeFOREST BOGART)

Born New York, N.Y., January 23, 1899. Educated Trinity School, New York; Phillips Academy, Andover, Massachusetts. Married (1) Helen Mencken, 1926 (divorced, 1928); (2) Mary Phillips, 1928 (divorced, 1938); (3) Mayo Methot, 1938 (divorced, 1945); (4) Lauren Bacall, 1945, children Stephen, Leslie. Academy award for best actor, 1951 (*The African Queen*). Served with U.S. Navy, World War I. Height 5′7″; weight 150 lb; dark brown hair, dark brown eyes. Sign: Aquarius. Died January 14, 1957.

"There wasn't a drop of theatrical blood in me," recalled Humphrey Bogart, probably the number-one screen tough of all time. The snarling ne'er-do-well of so many celluloid fisticuffs and shootouts was born in New York City, where his father was a well-to-do doctor. Bogart received fashionable schooling at New

Gangster, Warner Brothers style, ca. 1938

With Bette Davis in Marked Woman *(1937)*

With Lauren Bacall in The Big Sleep *(1946)*

York's Trinity School and the Phillips Academy in Massachusetts. This early in life, the nonconformist personality that became so familiar to the public was developing, and he was expelled from Phillips after a prank that failed to amuse his superiors.

Unwelcome at other schools, Bogart entered the navy and served in World War I on the troopship *Leviathan,* where a wood splinter found its way to his lip, leaving a permanent scar. Back in civvies, he found a theatrical post through a neighbor, producer William Brady, and made his Broadway bow in a two-line bit in *Drifting* (1920). Romantic juvenile roles (believe it or not) followed, and despite consistently poor reviews, he was in shows such as *Meet the Wife* (1923), *Cradle Snatchers* (1925), *Baby Mine* (1927), and *It's a Wise Child* (1929).

There were a number of false starts in the movies for Bogart. His first actual film was a rather dismal short subject called *Broadway's like That* (1930) with singer Ruth Etting. Fox talent scouts spotted him in *It's a Wise Child* and offered him a movie contract; six unspectacular pictures later, he was back east. With the depression in full force, he returned to the film colony for a variety of unmemorable films (for example, *Love Affair,* 1932, *Big City Blues,* 1932). This time when he again went back to New York, he swore he would never make another picture.

In 1935, Bogart was a hit on Broadway in *The Petrified Forest.* Playing the vicious gangster Duke Mantee, he made the role his own—cool, rough, and ruthless. Warner Brothers bought the screen rights, signing Leslie Howard to recreate his stage role opposite Bette Davis; the role of Mantee was intended for Warner's favorite, Edward G. Robinson, but Howard was so upset that his friend Bogart was being bypassed that he threatened to quit the project. Thus Bogart was cast in the picture.

With Katharine Hepburn in
The African Queen *(1951)*

From the time that Bogart entered the dingy café in *The Petri-fied Forest* (1936), he became one of the most distinctive and enjoyable of film players. Warner Brothers, seeing him as a splendid addition to the bullet-spitting racketeer yarns that earned them high revenue, signed him to a contract. For a while, he was cast as a trigger-happy, sneering, glowering heavy who was usually killed on screen by a gunshot or the electric chair. Some pictures, like *Dead End* (1937) for United Artists, and *Kid Galahad* (1937) and *The Roaring Twenties* (1939) for Warner's, were top entertainment, but others were simply showcases for tommy guns and wisecracks. "I was the Little Lord Fauntleroy of the lot," reminisced Bogart. "I played more scenes writhing around on the floor than I did standing up."

There were better times ahead. Both Paul Muni and George Raft refused the script of *High Sierra* (1941), the story of an aging, sympathetic gangster. Bogart got the part on the second rebound and played it with enough skill to earn a new evaluation by the critics and public. Later Raft declined another role that subsequently went to Bogart, the part of detective Sam Spade in the classic *Maltese Falcon* (1941). Abetted by the resourceful Mary Astor as the deceptive "heroine" and by the delightfully villainous Sydney Greenstreet and Peter Lorre, Bogart became a top star. "I had a lot going for me in that one," he said. "I don't have many things I'm proud of . . . but that's one of them."

In 1943, Bogart became king of the Warner lot and one of the top ten box-office attractions through his role in *Casablanca,* one of the most perennially popular movies ever made. As Rick, the cynical, bitter, gin-joint proprietor, he fully developed the Bogart-style hero—tough on the surface, strong in character, brutally honest, yet somehow lost and always romantic. His electric love

With Dooley Wilson and Ingrid Bergman in Casablanca (1943)

scenes with Ingrid Bergman were memorable, as were his witty, dry exchanges with suave police officer Claude Rains.

Now that Bogart was an established movie success, a series of roguish-hero roles followed, along with top salaries and billing. During *To Have and to Have Not* (1945), forty-six-year-old Bogart worked with eighteen-year-old starlet Lauren Bacall; the on-screen chemistry mixed just as well offscreen and she became his fourth wife (following his three unhappy marriages to other actresses). *The Big Sleep* (1946) saw him again as a detective, *Dark Passage* (1947) had him break out of San Quentin, and *Key Largo* (1948) found him in a thrilling exchange of bullets with Edward G. Robinson; in all three pictures, the leading lady was Lauren Bacall. During this time, Bogart established his own production company, Santana Productions, named after the yacht he enjoyed sailing.

There were other unforgettable Bogart characterizations. He was superb in *The Treasure of Sierra Madre* (1948) as the braggart Fred C. Dobbs who was driven insane by a lust for gold in the wilds of the Mexican mountains. In 1951, he won an Oscar for his performance as the whiskered, hard-drinking, belching, and totally engaging boatman in *The African Queen,* costarring with prim Katharine Hepburn. An equally memorable performance was as Captain Queeg, the paranoid navy captain who breaks under court-martial questioning in *The Caine Mutiny* (1954).

Stricken with throat cancer, Bogart died on January 14, 1957; his last film had been *The Harder They Fall* (1956). His survivors included his wife and two children. John Huston, who had frequently directed Bogart and who was a personal friend, eulogized him thus: "He was endowed with the greatest gift a man can have—talent. The whole world came to recognize it. . . . He is quite irreplaceable. There will never be another like him."

Films

1930: A Devil with Women, Up the River. *1931:* Body and Soul, Bad Sister, Women of All Nations, A Holy Terror. *1932:* Love Affair, Big City Blues, Three on a Match. *1934:* Midnight. *1936:* The Petrified Forest, Bullets or Ballots. Two against the World, China Clipper, Isle of Fury. *1937:* Black Legion, The Great O'Malley, Marked Woman, Kid Galahad, San Quentin, Dead End, Stand-In. *1938:* Swing Your Lady, Crime School, Men Are Such Fools, The Amazing Dr. Clitterhouse, Racket Busters, Angels with

Dirty Faces. *1939:* King of the Underworld, The Oklahoma Kid, Dark Victory, You Can't Get Away with Murder, The Roaring Twenties, The Return of Dr. X, Invisible Stripes. *1940:* Virginia City, It All Came True, Brother Orchid, They Drive by Night. *1941:* High Sierra, The Wagons Roll at Night, The Maltese Falcon. *1942:* All through the Night, The Big Shot, Across the Pacific. *1943:* Casablanca, Action in the North Atlantic, Thank Your Lucky Stars, Sahara. *1944:* Passage to Marseille. *1945:* To Have and to Have Not, Conflict. *1946:* Two Guys from Milwaukee,* The Big Sleep. *1947:* Dead Reckoning, The Two Mrs. Carrolls, Dark Passage. *1948:* Always Together,* The Treasure of Sierra Madre, Key Largo. *1949:* Knock on Any Door, Tokyo Joe. *1950:* Chain Lightning, In a Lonely Place. *1951:* The Enforcer, Sirocco, The African Queen. *1952:* Deadline U.S.A. *1953:* Battle Circus, The Love Lottery.* *1954:* Beat the Devil, The Caine Mutiny, Sabrina, The Barefoot Contessa. *1955:* We're No Angels, The Left Hand of God, The Desperate Hours. *1956:* The Harder They Fall.

* Unbilled cameo

2. MARLON BRANDO
(MARLON BRANDO, JR.)

Born Omaha, Nebraska, April 3, 1924. Educated Libertyville High School, Illinois; Shattuck Military Academy, Minnesota; New School for Social Research, New York. Married (1) Anna Kashfi, 1957 (divorced, 1959), children Christian, Devi; (2) Movita Castenada, 1960 (divorced, 1961). Academy awards for best actor, 1954 (*On the Waterfront*) and 1972 (*The Godfather*). Height 5'10"; weight 170 lb; brown hair, gray eyes. Sign: Aries.

Marlon Brando was the first great antihero, the first highly praised "method actor," and the first performer to make mumbling theatrically acceptable. An unpredictable artist, whose performances have ranged from brilliance to boorishness, Brando is still a major screen personality despite the fact that he is outrageously

In The Appaloosa *(1966)*

Marlon Brando in 1954

With Vivien Leigh in A Streetcar
Named Desire (1951)

difficult, sporadically good professionally, and extremely derogatory about acting as an art.

Born in Nebraska and raised in Illinois, Brando attended various schools before leaving to become a tile-fitter for a local drainage construction firm. His father saw this as an unpromising occupation and staked his son to a professional training course of his choice; Brando selected acting. (His mother operated the Omaha Community Playhouse, where Henry Fonda first appeared onstage.) He packed up and went to New York, studying with success at the Dramatic Workshop of the New School for Social Research.

Broadway first saw Brando in *I Remember Mama,* in which he played a fifteen-year-old and gained critical notice. After increasingly good roles in *Truckline Cafe, Candida,* and *A Flag Is Born,* Brando made theater history on December 12, 1947, in Tennessee Williams's drama *A Streetcar Named Desire.* His performance was heralded as being "like nothing else ever played."

Hollywood took note, and Marlon made his movie debut, starring in *The Men* (1950) as a crippled veteran attempting to adjust to civilian life. He followed up this success by recreating the character of Stanley Kowalski in the movie version of *A Streetcar Named Desire* (1951) with touching Vivien Leigh as his costar. The *New York Times* wrote that Brando "carries over all the energy and the steel spring characterization that made him vivid on the stage." Brando was nominated for an Oscar, but Humphrey Bogart won it that year for *The African Queen.*

A run of cinema hits followed. *Viva Zapata!* (1952) cast Brando as a Mexican rebel, and *Julius Caesar* (1953) joined him with an all-star cast (James Mason, Greer Garson, Deborah Kerr, and others)

With Katy Jurado, Karl Malden,
and Pina Pellicer in One-Eyed
Jacks (1961)

With Maria Schneider in
Last Tango in Paris (1973)

as bare-chested Marc Antony. *The Wild One* (1954) provided him with the leather-jacketed, motorcycle-riding hipster character that his cult would so gleefully extol. Brando's "method" approach to acting, with lots of scratching and slurred lines, made him a controversial and unique star in the Hollywood of this period.

Brando won his first Oscar for *On the Waterfront* (1954), in the role of a beleaguered striker who spoke the famous line, "I coulda' been a contender." Thereafter for a while, his output was an uneven mixture of mild successes and dismal flops. *Desiree* (1954) cast him as a mixed-up Napoleon with Jean Simmons as his love interest. *Guys and Dolls* (1955) starred him as a gambler who sang (!) "Luck Be a Lady" and other tunes. *The Teahouse of the August Moon* (1956) and *Sayonara* (1957) cast him in Oriental backgrounds and gave the meaty roles to others (Paul Ford and Red Buttons, respectively).

Brando tried his hand at directing with *One-Eyed Jacks* (1961), a western epic in which he also starred. It was a mess. He returned to just acting in *Mutiny on the Bounty* (1962), in which he managed to portray Fletcher Christian (one of Clark Gable's most enduring performances) as a dandified fop. During production, Marlon's temperament and antics nearly pushed MGM into bankruptcy. The rest of the sixties saw Brando doing bad imitations of himself in projects like *Bedtime Story* (1964), *The Chase* (1966), *The Countess from Hong Kong* (1967) (Charlie Chaplin's lamentable return to directing), and *Reflections in a Golden Eye* (1967), in which he played the homosexual husband of Elizabeth Taylor.

The public and producers had lost patience with Brando, who by the 1970s appeared to most people to be in total decline. However, director Francis Ford Coppola salvaged the Brando mystique by casting him in the title role of *The Godfather* (1972), the fabulously successful film version of the best-selling novel. Lauded as "the *Gone With the Wind* of the gangster films," the picture made Brando a respected name again as he played the jut-jawed, aged Mafia czar who never forgets his family. It is Oscar history now that Brando refused the award that the academy voted him because of what he considered the shabby treatment that the American Indian had received at the hands of Hollywood. An "Indian girl" mounted the stage and explained Brando's choice to a salvo of boos from the audience. She said that he was en route to observe the current difficulties with Indians at Wounded Knee, South Dakota, but he never arrived there.

Last Tango in Paris (1973), a European product termed a "moving experience" or "overblown pornography," depending on what critic you believe, kicked another goal for Brando. Once again, the man was at the peak of his profession.

Brando has twice married. In 1957, he wed Anna Kashfi, an Indian girl from Calcutta, and two children came of that two-year union. In 1960, he wed Mexican native Movita Castenada, a relationship that again resulted in divorce. The actor is active in civil rights causes, lives on an island in Tahiti, punches photographers, and still insists after earning (and wasting) millions of dollars that "Acting is a bum's life."

Films

1950: The Men. *1951:* A Streetcar Named Desire. *1952:* Viva Zapata! *1953:* Julius Caesar. *1954:* The Wild One, On the Waterfront, Desiree. *1955:* Guys and Dolls. *1956:* The Teahouse of the August Moon. *1957:* Sayonara. *1958:* The Young Lions. *1960:* The Fugitive Kind. *1961:* One-Eyed Jacks (also director). *1962:* Mutiny on the Bounty. *1963:* The Ugly American. *1964:* Bedtime Story. *1965:* The Saboteur: Code Name Morituri. *1966:* The Chase, The Appaloosa. *1967:* A Countess from Hong Kong, Reflections in a Golden Eye. *1968:* The Night of the Following Day, Candy. *1970:* Burn! *1972:* The Nightcomers, The Godfather. *1973:* Last Tango in Paris.

3. GARY COOPER

(FRANK JAMES COOPER)

Born Helena, Montana, May 7, 1901. Educated Wesleyan College, Montana; Grinnell College, Iowa. Married Veronica Balfe, 1933, child Maria. Academy awards for best actor, 1941 (*Sergeant York*) and 1952 (*High Noon*). Height 6'3"; weight 180 lb; brown hair, blue eyes. Sign: Taurus. Died May 13, 1961.

During his more than thirty-five years as a Hollywood movie player, Gary Cooper demonstrated that an innate ability to convey a natural manner could turn a performer into a major box-office draw. Although he won two academy awards, his acting style never reached any sophisticated level. It did not have to, for as long as he "portrayed" himself on screen, moviegoers were more than satisfied.

Cooper was born in Helena, Montana, where his father was a

With Marlene Dietrich in Morocco *(1930)*

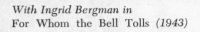

court clerk and later a Montana supreme-court justice. When he was nine, Frank James (Gary's given names) moved with his family to England, but they returned four years later when World War I erupted. Cooper went to high school in Helena, later attending Montana's Wesleyan College and Grinnell College in Iowa.

Art was Cooper's favorite subject, and after leaving college, he became a cartoonist for a Helena newspaper. However, his attempts to crash the art world of Chicago were unsuccessful, and he rejoined his parents, who had moved to California. Only after a failing attempt to succeed in the business world did he begin working in movies as a cowboy extra.

At the suggestion of his agent, Cooper changed his first name to Gary, and soon he was chosen by Samuel Goldwyn to support Ronald Colman and Vilma Banky in *The Winning of Barbara Worth*. The role was small, but the scenario provided that the character played by Cooper die in Colman's arms. *Motion Picture* magazine wrote, "Cooper played the most consistent and convincing characterization of the picture." Goldwyn offered him a $65-a-week contract, but Paramount had a better deal, placing a $165-a-week bid.

There were a number of formats for Cooper for which he developed his "natural" screen style. He was leading man to Clara Bow in *Children of Divorce* (1927) and to Lupe Velez (an off-screen romance for a time) in *Wolf Song* (1929). He played in the lushly mounted World War I aviation drama *Wings* (1927) and had the title role in *The Virginian* (1929), in which he spoke to villainous Walter Huston the famous line, "When you call me that . . . smile!"

By 1930, Cooper was an established box-office name, starring opposite such Paramount actresses as Marlene Dietrich in *Morocco*

With Dorothy McGuire and Tony Perkins in Friendly Persuasion *(1956)*

(1930), Carole Lombard in *I Take This Woman* (1931), Claudette Colbert in *His Woman* (1931), Tallulah Bankhead in *Devil and the Deep* (1932), and Helen Hayes in *A Farewell to Arms* (1932).

In 1933, Cooper wed Veronica Balfe, a socialite who had made a brief foray into movies under the name Sandra Shaw. Their only child, Maria, was born in 1937.

By the mid-thirties, Cooper was earning $6,000 a week on his Paramount contract and starring in some splendid features. *The Lives of a Bengal Lancer* (1935) was a rowdy adventure story that proved tremendously popular.

In *Mr. Deeds Goes to Town* (1936), directed by Frank Capra, Cooper found his true forte in the part of Longfellow Deeds, the country rube who inherits $20 million and has a tough time convincing a big-city court that his humanitarian ways should make sense to anyone. He was nominated for an Oscar for this "pixilated" performance. *Beau Geste* (1939), a foreign legion adventure tale, cast him in the stalwart title role, withstanding the attacks of Arabs and suffering the cruelty of martinet Brian Donlevy. This picture concluded his studio pact, and the much-in-demand actor free-lanced throughout the rest of his career.

Cooper estimated his talents by saying, "To get folks to like you, I figured you sort of had to be their ideal. I don't mean a handsome knight riding a white horse, but a fellow who answered the description of a right guy." *Sergeant York* (1941) proved this theory and won him an Oscar in the bargain. His sincere portrayal of the Tennessee farm boy who becomes a World War I hero was highly praised by critics and audiences alike.

Oscar nominations also rewarded Cooper's acting in *Pride of the Yankees* (1942), in which he played baseball great Lou Gehrig, and in *For Whom the Bell Tolls* (1943), which starred him with

In The Lives of a Bengal Lancer *(1935)*

Ingrid Bergman in a cinematization of his friend Ernest Heming-way's novel. Other films that kept Cooper a popular attraction throughout the forties were *Saratoga Trunk* (1945), De Mille's *Unconquered* (1947), a lavish, childish, rousing yarn of pre-Re-volutionary War days, and *The Fountainhead* (1948), the movie version of Ayn Rand's novel about an idealistic architect.

In Stanley Kramer's adult western *High Noon* (1952), Cooper received a role for which Gregory Peck had been mentioned— that of sheriff Will Kane. Not only was the film a huge success, but it earned Cooper his second Oscar and gave him renewed box-office life.

Cooper began to age noticeably after this film but maintained his status in films like *Vera Cruz* (1954), *Friendly Persuasion* (1956), and *The Hanging Tree* (1959). In 1960, he narrated a segment of NBC's "Project 20," entitled "The Real West," and traveled to England to star with Deborah Kerr in a suspense story, *The Naked Edge*.

By 1961, Cooper was bedridden; the ailment was stomach can-cer. That year he was awarded an honorary Oscar, which a teary James Stewart accepted for him. Said Stewart while Cooper watched at home, "We're all very proud of you, Coop. All of us are tremendously proud." When the news of his terminal illness was released two days later, thousands of letters, including messages from President Kennedy and Queen Elizabeth II, arrived at his Los Angeles home. He died on May 13, 1961. He was buried at Holy Cross Cemetery, but in 1973, his wife had his remains re-moved and buried under a boulder in "Gatsby County," Long Island, an area he had greatly loved.

In the late sixties, *Variety* conducted a poll of the most popular motion-picture stars, and both Cooper and Clark Gable (through television showings of their old movies) were still high on the list. Had he been alive, Cooper might have repeated his own assess-ment of his film popularity: "People ask me how come you've been around so long. Well, it's through playing the part of Mr. Average Joe American."

Films

1926: The Winning of Barbara Worth. *1927:* Arizona Bound, Ne-vada, The Last Outlaw, It, Children of Divorce, Wings. *1928:* Beau Sabreur, The Legion of the Condemned, Doomsday, Half a Bride, Lilac Time, The First Kiss, The Shopworn Angel. *1929:* Wolf Song,

Betrayal, The Virginian. *1930:* Only the Brave, The Texan, Seven Days' Leave, A Man from Wyoming, The Spoilers, Morocco. *1931:* Fighting Caravans, I Take This Woman, His Woman. *1932:* Devil and the Deep, If I Had a Million, A Farewell to Arms. *1933:* To-day We Live, One Sunday Afternoon, Design for Living, Alice in Wonderland, Operator 13. *1934:* Now and Forever, The Wedding Night. *1935:* The Lives of a Bengal Lancer, Peter Ibbetson. *1936:* Desire, Mr. Deeds Goes to Town, The General Died at Dawn, The Plainsman. *1937:* Souls at Sea. *1938:* The Adventures of Marco Polo, Bluebeard's Eighth Wife, The Cowboy and the Lady. *1939:* Beau Geste, The Real Glory. *1940:* The Westerner, North West Mounted Police. *1941:* Meet John Doe, Sergeant York, Ball of Fire. *1942:* Pride of the Yankees. *1943:* For Whom the Bell Tolls. *1944:* The Story of Dr. Wassell, Casanova Brown. *1945:* Along Came Jones, Saratoga Trunk. *1946:* Cloak and Dagger. *1947:* Uncon-quered. *1948:* Good Sam, The Fountainhead. *1949:* Task Force. *1950:* Bright Leaf, Dallas. *1951:* You're in the Navy Now, It's a Big Country, Distant Drums. *1952:* High Noon, Springfield Rifle. *1953:* Return to Paradise, Blowing Wild. *1954:* Garden of Evil, Vera Cruz. *1955:* The Court-Martial of Billy Mitchell. *1956:* Friendly Persuasion. *1957:* Love in the Afternoon. *1958:* Ten North Fred-erick, Man of the West. *1959:* The Hanging Tree, They Came to Cordura, The Wreck of the Mary Deare. *1961:* The Naked Edge.

4. JAMES DEAN

Born Fairmount, Indiana, February 8, 1931. Educated UCLA. Height 5′9″; weight 150 lb; light brown hair, gray eyes. Sign: Aquarius. Died September 30, 1955 in an automobile accident near Paso Robles, California.

James Dean's image of a rebellious youth, supported by his tragic and premature death, has made his memory that of a subculture idol. The hordes that ballyhooed him into a legend were far more responsible for his lasting popularity than was his acting. Or, as Humphrey Bogart said, "It's a good thing he died. He couldn't possibly have lived up to his reputation."

Dean was born in Fairmount, Indiana. His mother died when he was nine, and the boy was raised by an aunt. He participated in high-school theatricals and eventually won the Indiana State

James Dean at age 24

James Dean in 1955

With Julie Harris in East of Eden
(1955)

Dramatics Contest because of an effectively delivered monologue.

To follow up on his interest in acting, Dean went to UCLA, joining on the side a theater group run by actor James Whitmore. From this came bits in two forgettable movies, *Fixed Bayonets* (1951) and *Has Anybody Seen My Gal?* (1952). When Hollywood no longer appeared interested, Dean went to New York to break into television, but again only bit work was obtainable. At this time, he also appeared in a flop play, *See the Jaguar* (1952).

The "discovery" of Dean occurred when he appeared in the play version of André Gide's *The Immoralist* (1954). His role of a boy Arab lover not above blackmailing won him the notice of director Elia Kazan. Then preparing to direct *East of Eden,* the John Steinbeck story of alienated youth, Kazan recognized in the young actor the qualities necessary for the leading role of the "mixed-up kid." *East of Eden* (1955) had a powerful cast. Julie Harris played the charismatic girl; Raymond Massey was the disagreeable father. But Dean attracted most notice, creating perhaps the most definitive rebellious-youth performance ever captured on film. Warner Brothers realized they had a gold mine in Dean and quickly arranged another script for his moody talents. *Rebel without a Cause* (1955) was an entertaining picture that pitted the Dean rebel against tremendous odds—uncomprehending parents, a new school, and a hostile pack of punks complete with leather jackets and switchblades. Natalie Wood was his gentle girlfriend, Sal Mineo his peaceful pal. They became a sympathetic triumvirate to millions of unhappy, empathizing teen-agers.

Warner's had an epic at hand in *Giant* (1956) and was enlisting top talent to fill the major roles. Elizabeth Taylor and Rock Hudson were contracted, and Alan Ladd was originally scheduled to join them. However, Ladd's wife, always his professional adviser,

In the documentary, The James Dean Story *(1957)*

With Natalie Wood in Rebel without a Cause *(1955)*

talked him out of performing the part, and it was given to Dean. The role was that of a surly ranchhand who becomes an equally surly oil baron, aging throughout the picture. The *New York Times* said, "James Dean makes the malignant role . . . the most tangy and corrosive in the film. Mr. Dean plays that curious villain with a stylized spookiness—a sly sort of off-beat languor and slur of language—that concentrates spite. This is a haunting capstone of the brief career of Mr. Dean." Some agreed that the young actor held his own against the more experienced stars; other felt that Ladd, no great actor, could not have been worse. Dean was nevertheless nominated for an Oscar but lost it to Ernest Borgnine, of *Marty.* Dean was not a cooperative actor, and his disposition was arrogant. On all three starring films, he clashed with his directors, none of whom was reputed to be unreasonable.

A day after completing work on *Giant,* Dean was driving his new Porsche when he collided head on with an approaching car and was killed instantly. The ensuing idolatry nearly eclipsed the hysteria that took place after Valentino's death. *Rebel without a Cause* and *Giant* drew enormous receipts mainly because of the Dean name. Warner Brothers was showered with letters and photo requests. Two years after the fatal accident, the epidemic of rumors (lasting to this day) claimed that he was not dead at all but actually a "basket case," remotely hidden away to disguise his worse-than-death fate. To cash in on the uncommon interest in the actor, in 1957 Warner Brothers released a documentary called *The James Dean Story.*

The James Dean cult, although considerably shrunken, does continue. In fact, biographies from major publishers continue to pour forth, covering the star's brief life and quick career. There is, however, evidence that the fans are glorifying a false idol. Although Dean represented the young innocent plagued by ignorance and a cruel adult world, his old mentor Elia Kazan recalls that Dean himself was a "pudding of hatred."

Films

1951: Sailor Beware, Fixed Bayonets. *1952:* Has Anybody Seen My Gal? *1955:* East of Eden, Rebel without a Cause. *1956:* Giant. *1957:* The James Dean Story (documentary).

5. CLINT EASTWOOD

Born San Francisco, California, May 31, 1930. Educated Oakland Technical High School, California, Los Angeles City College. Married Maggie Johnson, 1953, children Kyle, Allison. Served with U.S. Army, 1948 to 1953. Height 6'4"; weight 190 lb; brown hair, green eyes. Sign: Gemini.

In an era when true heroes who always win and win big are just short of a vanishing breed, Clint Eastwood's towering frame stands almost alone. Born in San Francisco, he began life traveling a great deal, as his father took work where and when he could find it. After he graduated from high school, Eastwood enlisted in the army and was stationed at Fort Ord, California. He served as a swimming instructor and recalls numerous occasions on which he had to fish out an inductee who would otherwise have drowned.

It was at Fort Ord that Eastwood was spotted by a Universal-International assistant director who took note of the soldier's lanky

In A Fistful of Dollars *(1964)*

In Paint Your Wagon *(1969)*

With Jessica Walter in Play Misty for Me *(1971)*

good looks. After his discharge, the would-be actor called at Universal, only to learn that his contact was no longer on the studio payroll. As a result, Eastwood put aside his acting hopes temporarily and enrolled at Los Angeles City College, obtaining a part-time gas-station-mechanic job on the side. During this unglamorous period, he married Maggie Johnson, a blond model he had met on a blind date.

Los Angeles City College's business administration courses made Eastwood balk at the thought of a businessman's life, and on a dare, he arranged a Universal screen test. To his amazement, the studio saw promise in his tall, lanky physique and penetrating green eyes and signed him to a $75-a-week, forty-week-a-year contract. Unfortunately, Eastwood was lost in the shuffle at the studio busy promoting Rock Hudson and Tony Curtis, and he played unspectacular roles in drab films like *Revenge of the Creature* (1955), *Francis in the Navy* (1955), *Lady Godiva* (1955), and *Never Say Goodbye* (1956).

Universal soon dropped their unheralded "find," and he went over to RKO for two films, *The First Traveling Saleslady* (1956) and *Escapade in Japan* (1957). Thereafter film jobs were scarce, and Eastwood found himself digging swimming pools for eating money. Two acting jobs he did land were in *Ambush at Cimarron Pass* (1958) ("the lousiest western ever made," says Clint) and *Lafayette Escadrille* (1958), so poor a film that it convinced the veteran director William Wellman to embrace retirement.

Luck presented itself in 1958 when Eastwood was visiting a friend at CBS Television City. Robert Sparks, a national executive, saw him as a potential costar with Eric Fleming for the new series "Rawhide." Examination of his résumé and a new screen test resulted in Eastwood's seven-year stint as cattle driver Rowdy Yates

In Thunderbolt and Lightfoot
(1974)

in the popular series that made its debut in January, 1959.

In the spring of 1964, Eastwood's next push to major stardom occurred. His agent called and presented him with the offer of $15,000 to go to Spain to star in a German-Spanish-Italian coproduction with an Italian director. "I started laughing," Clint recalls. "No, I told him. I wouldn't want it. 'Read the script,' he said. Oh yeah. My curiosity is killing me. But I did read it and I got wrapped up in it." The result was *Per Un Perguna di Dollari*, which would be known in English-speaking countries as *A Fistful of Dollars*. In this feature, Eastwood created a "man with no name" character, taking advantage of a family feud or turning a town into a virtual cemetery, and he was a sensation. The "spaghetti western" earned over $7 million in European distribution alone.

Since this milestone picture, Eastwood has increased his luster through a series of taciturn, rugged, no-nonsense portrayals. He played variations on his no-name character in *Per Qualche Dollari in Piu* (*For a Few Dollars More*) and *The Good, the Bad, and the Ugly*. By the time the third picture was made, Clint could demand and get, "$250,000 plus 10 percent of the Western world profits." Although made in 1964 and 1965, these films did not appear in America until 1967. When they did, however, the box-office impact was terrific.

Since then, Eastwood has been in the top ten attractions of American cinema. *Hang 'em High,* a rugged western in which Clint survives a hanging, and *Coogan's Bluff,* starring him as an Arizona sheriff stalking his prey to Manhattan, were released in 1968. (The latter was the first of several Eastwood pictures directed by action specialist Don Siegel.) In 1969 he costarred with Richard Burton in *Where Eagles Dare,* a World War II adventure yarn, and *Paint*

With Eli Wallach in The Good, the Bad, and the Ugly *(1966)*

Your Wagon, a boisterous musical in which his singing merited no such future assignments. There were two Eastwood films in 1970, *Kelly's Heroes,* another war escapade, and *Two Mules for Sister Sara,* which cast him as a cold yet compassionate cowpoke with Shirley MacLaine (replacing Elizabeth Taylor) as a whore in nun's clothing.

After starring in *The Beguiled* (1971), a Civil War story that proved too arty for the moviegoing public, Eastwood made his directorial debut with *Play Misty for Me* (1971), in which he also starred as a Monterey-area disc jockey pursued by a homicidal maniac (Jessica Walter). Since then he has directed *Breezy* (1973), an April-October love story, and *High Plains Drifter* (1973), a modern sagebrush allegory of revenge, both flops.

Eastwood's most popular role recently has been as Harry Callahan, the tough maverick detective in *Dirty Harry* (1971) and *Magnum Force* (1973), both box-office winners. Reviewing the former, *Time* observed, "[he] gives his best performance so far— tense, tough, full of implicit identification with his character."

Eastwood's *Thunderbolt and Lightfoot* (1974), which delighted exhibitors, and *The Eiger Sanction,* which he directed and starred in, indicate that continued stardom is his. A major sex symbol of the American cinema, he nevertheless maintains a private relatively simple life, dividing his time between two homes, one in the San Fernando Valley and one in Carmel, California. For relaxation he enjoys jogging, riding his motorcycle and pick-up truck, and playing pool and tennis. He and his wife annually host the Clint Eastwood Invitational Tennis Tournament at Pebble Beach.

For such a valuable commodity, Clint is exceedingly modest. He insists that "whatever success I've had is a lot of instinct and a little luck. I just go by how I feel."

Films

1955: Revenge of the Creature, Francis in the Navy, Lady Godiva, Tarantula. *1956:* Never Say Goodbye, The First Traveling Saleslady, Star in the Dust. *1957:* Escapade in Japan. *1958:* Ambush at Cimarron Pass, Lafayette Escadrille. *1964:* A Fistful of Dollars. *1965:* For a Few Dollars More. *1966:* The Good, the Bad, and the Ugly. *1967:* The Witches (in the episode: A Night like Any Other). *1968* Hang 'em High. *1969:* Coogan's Bluff, Where Eagles Dare,

Paint Your Wagon. *1970:* Kelly's Heroes, Two Mules for Sister Sara. *1971:* The Beguiled, Play Misty for Me (also director), Dirty Harry. *1972:* Joe Kidd, High Plains Drifter (also director). *1973:* Breezy (director only), Magnum Force. *1974:* Thunderbolt and Lightfoot. *1975:* The Eiger Sanction (also director).

6. ERROL FLYNN

Born Hobart, Tasmania, June 20, 1909. Educated in private schools, England and Australia. Married (1) Lili Damita, 1935 (divorced, 1943), child Sean; (2) Nora Eddington, 1943 (divorced, 1949), children Deidre, Rory; (3) Patrice Wymore, 1950. Height 6'1"; weight 175 lb; light brown hair, hazel eyes. Sign: Gemini. Died October 14, 1959 in Vancouver, British Columbia.

Errol Flynn's unique devil-may-care attitude on screen was matched only by his flamboyantly go-to-hell philosophy off screen. Rarely, if ever, has a cinema star had such a scandal-ridden private life or one so incongruously in juxtaposition to his heroic, gentlemanly image.

Flynn was born in Tasmania, the only child of a famous marine biologist. His wealthy family sent him to exclusive private schools in England, Australia, and Paris, but his stays there usually ended

In The Charge of the Light Brigade *(1936)*

With *Olivia de Havilland* in The
Adventures of Robin Hood *(1938)*

With *Bette Davis* in The Private
Lives of Elizabeth and Essex
(1939)

in decidedly dishonorable expulsion. At seventeen, he ran away
from his domineering mother and submissive father to seek a life
of adventure. He found it.

Flynn traveled to New Guinea and investigated the gold rush
there, wandering through the jungles and occasionally fighting the
natives. He would later recall with an amused nostalgia the beau-
tiful women he bedded (frequently the wives of employers), the
danger of his work, and the diseases (malaria and syphilis among
them) that he battled during his exceedingly lighthearted early
years.

While he was in New Guinea, Flynn as a lark appeared in a
film as a member of *Dr. H. Erbin's New Guinean Expedition*
(1932), which in turn led to his being cast in the makeshift *In the
Wake of the Bounty* (1933). Attracted by the novel idea of becoming a professional actor, the handsome young man journeyed
to England to heed his new whim. He landed a berth with the
Northampton Repertory Company, and during the group's partici-
pation at the Stratford Summer Festival, he was spotted by a talent
agent for the British division of Warner Brothers. He was signed
to a $150-a-week contract and made his official debut in *Murder
at Monte Carlo* (1934).

Jack L. Warner's company then shifted its new player to the
Burbank studio, where the best they could, or would, offer him
was the role of a corpse in *The Case of the Curious Bride* (1935),
in which Warren William played lawyer Perry Mason. But such
indignities were not to last. In 1935, because of a bargaining mis-
understanding, Warner's lost the services of Englishman Robert
Donat, who was to star in the studio's big-budgeted *Captain
Blood*. With a large cast, a full crew, and expensive sets waiting,

With Alexis Smith in Gentleman
Jim (1942)

In Kim (1951)

the studio took a desperate chance and cast Flynn in the role.
The results were better than anyone had dared to hope. Not since
the days of Douglas Fairbanks, Sr., had there been a more dashing, inspiring, athletic, and swashbuckling romantic movie hero.
Besides finding an epic hero in Flynn and an epic villain in Basil
Rathbone as Flynn's foil-thrusting rival, the movie found an epic
heroine in Olivia de Havilland as Flynn's demure but spunky
romantic interest. The film set a profitable pattern that the studio
would often repeat.

Thereafter, Flynn became one of the highest paid, most fawned-
upon sex symbols of the Hollywood golden age. Warner's tried
him in a variety of formats cast opposite the studio's most popular
leading ladies, including Kay Francis, Joan Blondell, Bette Davis
(she despised him and vice versa), and, of course, de Havilland.
Among the rowdy, totally enjoyable films that Flynn starred in
were *The Charge of the Light Brigade* (1936); *The Sisters* (1938);
The Dawn Patrol (1938), the classic account of World War I
flyers on certain-death missions; *Dodge City* (1939), the first of
several westerns in which Flynn's English accent made him a different albeit convincing hero; *The Private Lives of Elizabeth and
Essex* (1939); *The Sea Hawk* (1940), another swashbuckler of
delightfully gaudy epic proportions; and *They Died with Their
Boots On* (1941), in which he played Custer.

No role fitted Flynn so handsomely as that of the hero of *The
Adventures of Robin Hood* (1938), shot in technicolor. He was
wholly captivating as the impudent, charming Robin, swinging
on vines through Sherwood Forest, eluding an entire castle of
villains, or winning an archery match by splitting the arrow of a
perfect bull's eye. Of course, de Havilland was Maid Marion and

the scoundrels included wicked Sir Guy of Gisbourne (Rathbone) and Prince John (Claude Rains).

Flynn's celluloid fame did not delight him. He resented the sneers of critics who lambasted his acting, disliked the boors who picked fights with him in public to test his toughness, and grew weary of formula films. His discontent took form in wild and often decadent behavior. "John Barrymore, John Carradine, and I used to go three or four days without sleeping," Flynn later recalled. The trio would carouse on land or sea, usually accompanied by an assortment of female company. Flynn's boisterous behavior caught up with him, or so it seemed, when in 1942, he was charged by two teen-aged girls with statutory rape. Although he was ac-quitted, the episode left Flynn the object of dirty jokes and lewd stories for years to come.

When World War II erupted, Flynn tried to enlist but was given 4-F status because of a heart already weakened by wild living. Instead, he won back-lot battles in films like *Desperate Journey* (1942), *Edge of Darkness* (1943), and *Objective, Burma!* (1945).

After the war, life was unhappy for Flynn. His film vehicles were less than satisfactory; they were mostly westerns like *San Antonio* (1945), romances like *Escape Me Never* (1947), and a return to sword play in *The Adventures of Don Juan* (1949). Away from Warner's, pictures like *Adventures of Captain Fabian* (1951) and *Crossed Swords* (1954) did not help.

Marriage did not help to stabilize him. In 1935, he had married Lili Damita, a volatile French actress by whom he had a son, Sean (missing in action in Vietnam); she divorced him in 1943. His sec-ond spouse, Nora Eddington, was a cigarette girl in the lobby of the courthouse where his rape trial took place. Their marriage lasted seven years and produced two offspring. After that union, Flynn wed actress Patrice Wymore, but by the mid-fifties, their relationship had faltered.

Flynn's waning show-business career was somewhat salvaged when he won critical acclaim, for once, as a boozer in *The Sun Also Rises* (1957). Warner Brothers recalled him to play his old crony John Barrymore in *Too Much, Too Soon* (1958), and Fox sent him to Africa to star as a dissipated drunk in *The Roots of Heaven* (1958). Along the way, he was the host of a television series, "The Errol Flynn Theater." But it was too late for a come-back; a heart attack claimed him on October 14, 1959, while he was in Vancouver trying to sell his yacht for badly needed funds.

Following Flynn's death and the posthumous publication of his

as-told-to autobiography, *My Wicked, Wicked Ways,* Beverly Aad-
land, the star's teen-age lover of his last days, sued his estate for
Flynn's alleged corruption of morals. The final indignity was that
Flynn (eulogized by Jack L. Warner as "the personification of
gallantry, the essence of bravery, the great adventurer") was
buried at Forest Lawn, a cemetery he had detested as garish and
overblown.

Films

1932: Dr. H. Erbin's New Guinean Expedition. *1933:* In the Wake
of the Bounty. *1935:* Murder at Monte Carlo, The Case of the
Curious Bride, Don't Bet on Blondes, Captain Blood. *1936:* The
Charge of the Light Brigade. *1937:* Green Light, The Prince and
the Pauper, Another Dawn, The Perfect Specimen. *1938:* The Ad-
ventures of Robin Hood, Four's a Crowd, The Sisters, The Dawn
Patrol. *1939:* Dodge City, The Private Lives of Elizabeth and
Essex. *1940:* Virginia City, The Sea Hawk, Santa Fe Trail. *1941:*
Footsteps in the Dark, Dive Bomber. *1942:* They Died with Their
Boots On, Desperate Journey, Gentleman Jim. *1943:* Edge of Dark-
ness, Thank Your Lucky Stars, Northern Pursuit. *1944:* Uncertain
Glory. *1945:* Objective, Burma! San Antonio. *1946:* Never Say
Goodbye. *1947:* Cry Wolf, Escape Me Never. *1948:* Silver River.
1949: The Adventures of Don Juan, It's a Great Feeling, That
Forsyte Woman. *1950:* Montana, Rocky Mountain. *1951:* Kim,
Hello God, Adventures of Captain Fabian. *1952:* Mara Maru,
Against All Flags. *1953:* The Master of Ballantrae. *1954:* Crossed
Swords, William Tell (not completed). *1955:* Let's Make Up, The
Warriors, King's Rhapsody. *1956:* Istanbul. *1957:* The Big Boodle,
The Sun Also Rises. *1958:* Too Much, Too Soon; The Roots of
Heaven. *1959:* Cuban Rebel Girls.

7. HENRY FONDA

(HENRY JAYNES FONDA)

Born Grand Island, Nebraska, May 16, 1905. Educated University of Minnesota. Married (1) Margaret Sullavan, 1931 (divorced, 1933), (2) Frances Brokaw, 1936 (died, 1950), children Jane, Peter; (3) Susan Blanchard, 1950 (divorced, 1956), child Amy; (4) Afdera Franchetti, 1957 (divorced, 1962); (5) Shirlee Adams, 1965. Served U.S. Navy, World War II. Height 6'1"; weight 175 lb; brown hair, blue eyes. Sign: Taurus.

Henry Fonda's acting résumé is possibly the most crammed and impressive of any major actor still active today. And he shows no signs of slowing down.

Fonda was born in Grand Island, Nebraska, where his father owned a printing company. His earliest ambition was to become a writer, and he entered the University of Minnesota to major in

In The Grapes of Wrath *(1940)*

journalism. Unfortunately, the family finances demanded that he work to pay the tuition, and an exhausted Henry left the school after two years.

It was at the insistence of Mrs. Marlon Brando, Sr., the mother of the famous actor, that Fonda joined the Omaha Community Theater. He had not given acting a thought, but he decided to try it, leaving an unexciting job with a retail credit company to do so. The play was *You and I*, and it was all Fonda required to convince him to follow a stage career. He spent three years with the Omaha group, completely stagestruck and usually unsalaried.

Thereafter Fonda turned to vaudeville; he appeared with the old Lincoln impersonator George Billinger in a sketch he wrote himself; worked in stock in New England; and joined the University Players, a stock company that included such future successes as Joshua Logan, Margaret Sullavan, and James Stewart. Fonda stayed for four years. On Broadway, he understudied and played bits in shows like *A Game of Love and Death* and *Forsaking All Others*, eventually landing a good comic part in *New Faces* (1934). Finally, he obtained the leading role of the farm boy in *The Farmer Takes a Wife* (1934), and at this success Hollywood beckoned.

The film version of *The Farmer Takes a Wife* (1935), in which Fonda costarred with then box-office favorite Janet Gaynor, was a fine introduction for the tall, soft-spoken young actor. Audiences immediately grasped his understated acting; his integrity was ever apparent. Thereafter he was busy accepting leading roles offered by several studios. Paramount costarred him with Sylvia Sidney in *Trail of the Lonesome Pine* (1936), the first outdoor picture in technicolor, and with Margaret Sullavan in *The Moon's Our Home* (1936). The publicity department had fun with this film, since Miss Sullavan and Fonda had been married and were now divorced. Warner Brothers gave him to Bette Davis as her leading man in *That Certain Woman* (1937) and *Jezebel* (1938), for which Miss Davis won her second Oscar. And United Artists starred him with Sylvia Sidney in *You Only Live Once* (1937), a widely acclaimed social drama.

It was 20th Century-Fox, however, that offered Henry his top successes. He created a classic western characterization with his tobacco-chewing, gun-slinging Frank James in the rowdy *Jesse James* (1939). Under director John Ford's guidance, he played Abe Lincoln in his early lawyer days in *Young Mr. Lincoln* (1939) and

With Janet Gaynor in The Farmer Takes a Wife *(1935)*

With James Stewart in Firecreek *(1968)*

joined Claudette Colbert in battling savage Indians and evil Tories in *Drums along the Mohawk* (1939). There followed perhaps his greatest screen performance—Tom Joad, an ex-con released from prison just in time to join his displaced Okie family in a heart-breaking trek to California in *The Grapes of Wrath* (1940). For this performance, Fonda was nominated for an Oscar and should have won it; but it went to James Stewart for *The Philadelphia Story.*

Fox had used the Joad role to ensnare Fonda into a long-term contract, and he spent much of the early forties battling studio chief Darryl F. Zanuck over suitable scripts. Fox's only truly memorable use of him was in the superb *Ox-Bow Incident* (1943); his other fine films of this time, *The Lady Eve* (1941) and *The Male Animal* (1942) were made on loan to other studios.

In 1942, Fonda entered the navy, declining a post as a training-film director in favor of active duty on a destroyer in the Pacific. He received a bronze star and a presidential citation when discharged as a lieutenant.

There were some good films for Fonda to appear in when he returned to Hollywood, notably John Ford's *My Darling Clementine* (1946) and *Fort Apache* (1948). But he felt more drawn to the stage, and on February 19, 1948, he began a three-year run in *Mr. Roberts,* the famous comedy of World War II life on a battleship. It has become one of the most often revived plays of all time, was made into a television series, and of course, is a film familiar to late-show enthusiasts. Fonda in the title role fell in love with the show and eventually toured in it, becoming a stage star of top proportions. There followed such Broadway hits as *Point of No Return* (1951) and *The Caine Mutiny Court Martial* (1955).

In 1955, Warner Brothers planned a film production of *Mr.*

With Jack Warden, Edward Binns,
E. G. Marshall, John Fiedler,
Ed Begley, Robert Webber, Jack
Klugman, George Voskovec, Martin
Balsam, and Joseph Sweeney in
Twelve Angry Men (1957)

Roberts, seeking William Holden or Marlon Brando to play the title character. Holden declined, feeling that the part belonged to Fonda, but Brando accepted. An outraged press and the director, Fonda's old pal John Ford, insisted that Fonda be reinstated, and he was. Unfortunately, Fonda and Ford clashed over the picture; Fonda complained when Ford injected what the star considered overly low comic relief, and reputedly a fistfight ensued. Shortly afterwards, Ford fell ill and was replaced by Mervyn LeRoy. *Mr. Roberts* was a big hit, and Fonda was again a screen name.

Since then, Fonda has been a high-priced, welcome fixture in films, the theater, and television. Some of his movies, like *Twelve Angry Men* (1957) and *Fail Safe* (1964), he is justifiably proud of; others, like *Sex and the Single Girl* (1964), he tackled to finance his lavish mode of living. Broadway has seen him in several plays —*Silent Night, Lonely Night; Two for the Seesaw; Critics' Choice; A Gift of Time; Generation;* and a revival of *Our Town.* On television, he has performed in adaptations of *The Petrified Forest* and *Arrowsmith,* portrayed famous clown Emmett Kelly on "G.E. Theater," and appeared in a sagebrush series, "The Deputy."

Fonda, whose children Jane and Peter have become show-business names in their own rights, has wed five times. His current wife, Shirlee, young and attractive, is considered by his friends and children to be ideal for him.

Now seventy, Fonda remains as energetic as ever, acting as a salesman for a camera product on television, starring with James Stewart or Elizabeth Taylor in films like *The Cheyenne Social Club* (1971) and *Ash Wednesday* (1973), and appearing on Broad-

In Mister Roberts *(1955)*

way, on tour, and on television in a one-man show as Clarence
Darrow. When all this activity became too physically taxing for
the star, he left the one-man show to have a pacemaker inserted in
his heart. He was back on stage within a week of the operation.

Films

1935: The Farmer Takes a Wife, Way Down East, I Dream Too
Much. *1936:* Trail of the Lonesome Pine, The Moon's Our
Home, Spendthrift. *1937:* Wings of the Morning, You Only Live
Once, Slim, That Certain Woman. *1938:* I Met My Love Again,
Jezebel, Blockade, Spawn of the North, The Mad Miss Manton.
1939: Jesse James, Let Us Live, The Story of Alexander Graham
Bell, Young Mr. Lincoln, Drums along the Mohawk. *1940:* The
Grapes of Wrath, Lillian Russell, The Return of Frank James,
Chad Hanna. *1941:* The Lady Eve, Wild Geese Calling, You Be-
long to Me. *1942:* The Male Animal, Rings on Her Fingers, The
Magnificent Dope, Tales of Manhattan, The Big Street. *1943:* The
Immortal Sergeant, The Ox-Bow Incident. *1946:* My Darling Clem-
entine. *1947:* The Long Night, The Fugitive, Daisy Kenyon. *1948:*
A Miracle Can Happen, Fort Apache. *1949:* Jigsaw. *1955:* Mr.
Roberts. *1956:* War and Peace. *1957:* The Wrong Man, The Tin
Star, Twelve Angry Men. *1958:* Stage Struck. *1959:* Warlock, The
Man Who Understood Women. *1962:* Advise and Consent, The
Longest Day. *1963:* How the West Was Won, Spencer's Moun-
tain. *1964:* The Best Man, Fail Safe, Sex and the Single Girl. *1965:*
The Rounders, In Harm's Way, Battle of the Bulge. *1966:* A Big
Hand for the Little Lady, The Dirty Game. *1967:* Welcome to
Hard Times. *1968:* Firecreek; Yours, Mine and Ours; Madigan;
The Boston Strangler. *1969:* Once Upon a Time in the West. *1970:*
Too Late the Hero, There Was a Crooked Man. *1971:* The Chey-
enne Social Club. *1973:* The Serpent, Ash Wednesday. *1974:* My
Name Is Nobody, Last Days of Mussolini. *1976:* Midway.

8. CLARK GABLE

(WILLIAM CLARK GABLE)

Born Cadiz, Ohio, February 1, 1901. Educated Edinburg High School. Married (1) Josephine Dillon, 1924 (divorced, 1939); (2) Ria Langham, 1930 (divorced, 1939); (3) Carole Lombard, 1939 (died, 1942); (4) Lady Sylvia Ashley, 1949 (divorced 1952); (5) Kay Williams Spreckels, 1955, child John Clark Gable, born posthumously. Academy award for best actor, 1934 (*It Happened One Night*). Served with U.S. Army Air Corps, 1942 to 1944. Height 6'1"; weight 200 lb; black hair, gray eyes. Sign: Aquarius. Died November 16, 1960.

Clark Gable, the most idolized film star of all time, was the only child of William and Adeline Gable, both of Dutch extraction. When he was seven months old, his mother died, and he was left in the care of a grandmother until he was nearly six. His father had by then remarried, and Gable remembered his stepmother as

With Yvonne De Carlo in Band of Angels *(1957)*

possibly the kindest of the many women in his life.

The Gables moved to Akron, where the teen-age Clark worked for Firestone Tire Co. Meanwhile, he was spending his spare time with a little-theater group. Eventually he became so stagestruck that he quit his job to become an unpaid page boy for the stock company, which sometimes rewarded him with bit parts. After a brief venture on Broadway as a page boy, Gable took a job in Oklahoma until he had saved enough money to join a repertory company.

In 1924, twenty-three-year-old Clark married forty-three-year-old director-drama coach Josephine Dillon. The couple went to Los Angeles, where after an unsatisfactory screen test (he was too much of a roughneck), Gable returned to little-theatre efforts. Finally, a meaty role in *The Last Mile*, a rugged prison play, called him to the attention of actor-director Lionel Barrymore, and Gable was asked to take another screen test. This began his Hollywood career in earnest. (He had previously done bit parts in silent movies.) His real moving-picture debut was as an ornery cowboy in *The Painted Desert* (1931). Not long afterward, he and Miss Dillon were divorced, and he wed another older woman, the twice-divorced, socially prominent Ria Langham. (Gable's marriages to women, not only older but also rather frumpy, were a great headache to the MGM publicity department.) The ingredient that most ensured Gable's screen success was his magnetic and rugged manliness, effectively demonstrated when he slugged Norma Shearer on camera in *A Free Soul* (1931). Indeed, Gable wasn't so much of a hero in his early roles as he was a brutally attractive heavy. "It was Clark who made villains popular. Instead of the audience wanting the good guy to get the girl, they wanted the heavy to win her," said Shearer, who chose Gable to be her leading man again, in the film versions of Eugene O'Neill's *Strange Interlude* (1932) and Robert Sherwood's *Idiot's Delight* (1939).

Metro-Goldwyn-Mayer head Louis B. Mayer sensed Gable's screen chemistry, and Gable soon replaced John Gilbert and Ramon Novarro as the studio's prime leading man. He played opposite Greta Garbo in *Susan Lennox—Her Fall and Rise* (1931), Marion Davies in *Polly of the Circus* (1932), and Mary Astor and Jean Harlow in *Red Dust* (1932).

In 1933, Gable became a top money-maker, and MGM was forced to raise his salary to $2,500 weekly. However, to penalize him for contractual demands, the studio loaned him to Columbia

Clark Gable in 1931

With Jean Harlow in Red Dust *(1932)*

for a quickie called *It Happened One Night* (1934) opposite Paramount's Claudette Colbert. Both initially saw the film as professional slumming, but they later relaxed under Frank Capra's expert direction. They were both amazed when they won academy awards for their work in this comedy about a runaway heiress and the newspaper man who tries to track her down.

During the thirties, Clark starred in such varied vehicles as the comedy *Forsaking All Others,* the adventure story *Call of the Wild,* the costume drama *Mutiny on the Bounty,* and the gangster film *Manhattan Melodrama.* His most famous role was that of the dashing Rhett Butler in the film version of Margaret Mitchell's mammoth Civil War novel *Gone With the Wind* (1939).(To date, this movie has grossed over $80 million in theater distribution and an additional $5 million for a special television showing.) Gable's performance is one of the reasons for its enduring popularity, despite the fact that he feared doing the role of Rhett. "He was too popular. . . . I didn't want the part for money, marbles, or chalk."

Also in 1939, he wed vivacious comedienne Carole Lombard, who became the most popular part of the Gable legend as we know it today. Their joyous union ended tragically in 1942 when on a war-bond selling tour, screen star Carole was killed in a Nevada plane crash. Shortly thereafter the grief-stricken Clark, at the age of forty-one, enlisted in the army. After graduating from officers' training school in the upper third of his class, he served as a machine gunner in bombing missions over Europe, winning the Distinguished Flying Cross and the Air Medal for "courage, coolness, and skill in five missions."

Following his discharge, Gable returned to films with the medi-

With Vivien Leigh in Gone With
the Wind (1939)

With Estelle Winwood, Eli
Wallach, Montgomery Clift, and
Marilyn Monroe in The Misfits
(1961)

ocre *Adventure* (1945), which was promoted with the slogan,
"Gable's back and [Greer] Garson's got him." It was not until
1947 that his next picture was released, this one a healthy box-
office champion, *The Hucksters*. Gable was never better than when
he dumped a pitcher of water on tycoon Sydney Greenstreet's head
in this slick exposé of the advertising world. In *Command Decision*
(1949), Gable used his wartime experience in a powerful portrayal
of an air-force general forced to send flyers on certain-death missions.

The postwar television era brought some disastrous changes to
the film industry, and Gable's image was tinkered with in a number of unsatisfactory features during the fifties. Exceptions were
three box-office winners—*Mogambo* (1953), *Soldier of Fortune*
(1955), and *The Tall Men* (1955), which supplied him with strong
manly roles and such outstanding leading ladies as Ava Gardner,
Grace Kelly, Susan Hayward, and Jane Russell.

In 1955, Gable married Kay Spreckels (following an unhappy
union with overly refined Lady Sylvia Ashley), who survived him
and by whom he had a posthumous son, John Clark, his only
child. His final film was *The Misfits* (1961), in which he played
opposite the much younger Marilyn Monroe. The location work
was demanding, the delays in filming taxing; Gable insisted on
doing his own stunts. Shortly after completion, he was stricken
with a coronary thrombosis. He died in Hollywood Presbyterian
Hospital on November 6, 1960.

John Huston, director of *The Misfits* said of Clark, "His career
in pictures had the same sweep and color as Dempsey's in the
ring. . . . He is the only screen actor I can think of who rated the

sobriquet, the King." It wasn't the eulogy that modest Gable expected. He once told a friend, "I can't emote worth a damn. When I die they'll put on my tombstone 'He was lucky—and he knew it!'"

Films

1924: Forbidden Paradise. *1925:* What Price Glory? The Pacemakers, The Merry Widow, The Plastic Age. *1926:* North Star. *1931:* The Painted Desert; The Easiest Way; Dance, Fools, Dance; The Secret Six; The Finger Points; Laughing Sinners; A Free Soul; Night Nurse; Sporting Blood; Susan Lennox—Her Fall and Rise; Possessed; Hell Divers. *1932:* Polly of the Circus, Red Dust, Strange Interlude, No Man of Her Own. *1933:* The White Sister, Hold Your Man, Night Flight, Dancing Lady. *1934:* It Happened One Night, Men in White, Manhattan Melodrama, Chained, Forsaking All Others. *1935:* After Office Hours, Call of the Wild, China Seas, Mutiny on the Bounty. *1936:* Wife vs. Secretary, San Francisco, Cain and Mabel, Love on the Run. *1937:* Parnell, Saratoga. *1938:* Test Pilot, Too Hot to Handle. *1939:* Idiot's Delight, Gone With the Wind. *1940:* Strange Cargo, Boom Town, Comrade X. *1941:* They Met in Bombay, Honky Tonk. *1942:* Somewhere I'll Find You. *1945:* Adventure. *1947:* The Hucksters. *1948:* Homecoming, Command Decision. *1949:* Any Number Can Play. *1950:* Key to the City, To Please a Lady. *1951:* Across the Wide Missouri, Callaway Went Thataway.* *1952:* Lone Star. *1953:* Never Let Me Go, Mogambo. *1954:* Betrayed. *1955:* Soldier of Fortune, The Tall Men. *1956:* The King and Four Queens. *1957:* Band of Angels. *1958:* Run Silent, Run Deep; Teacher's Pet. *1959:* But Not for Me. *1960:* It Started in Naples. *1961:* The Misfits.

* Unbilled cameo

9. ELLIOT GOULD

(ELLIOT GOLDSTEIN)

Born Brooklyn, New York, August 29, 1938. Educated Children's Professional School, New York City, Columbia College of Columbia University. Married (1) Barbra Streisand, 1963 (divorced, 1971), child Jason; (2) Jennifer Bogart, 1974 (separated), children Molly, Sam. Height 6'3"; weight 205 lb; black hair, brown eyes. Sign: Virgo.

"Pseudo-hysterics . . . have made Elliot Gould a star for an uptight age. In Gould they see all their tensions, frustrations, and insecurities personified and turned into nervous comedy that both tickles and stings with the shock of recognition." Thus wrote *Time* of the star of social satires like *Bob and Carol and Ted and Alice,* *M*A*S*H,* and *Little Murders.*

Born in Brooklyn, Elliot Goldstein grew up in a Jewish atmosphere worthy of Portnoy, moving during his adolescence to West

With Bibi Andersson in The Touch *(1971)*

With Jason Robards, Jr., in
The Night They Raided Minsky's
(1968)

With Natalie Wood in Bob and
Carol and Ted and Alice *(1969)*

Orange, New Jersey. His mother wanted a show-business career for him and pushed him into lessons in speech, singing, dancing, and drama. Soon she changed his name to Gould, and the boy began appearing on local television and network programs, including the "Colgate Comedy Hour." He also modeled and worked in dying vaudeville at the New York Palace Theater.

Gould went on to train at the Children's Professional School and Columbia College, and he made his Broadway debut in 1957 in *Rumble,* an unsuccessful musical. Such shows as *Say Darling* (1958) and *Irma La Douce* (1960) followed before Gould won the lead in *I Can Get It for You Wholesale* (1962). His reviews were less than enthusiastic, and a kid in a small part, Barbra Streisand, stole a considerable amount of his thunder. Gould apparently did not hold it against her; he married her in 1963 (they have a son by the marriage). They separated in 1969 and divorced in 1971.

Gould followed this play with other stage work, including touring with Liza Minnelli in *The Fantasticks,* appearing in London in *On the Town,* and starring in a Broadway fiasco, *Drat! The Cat!* He also starred in *Little Murders* (1967), Jules Feiffer's bloody satire that quickly folded, and he later toured with Shelley Winters in *Luv.*

Gould's first two films did little for him; they were *The Night They Raided Minsky's* (1968), and *The Confession,* filmed earlier in Jamaica but delayed in release. Then came *Bob and Carol and Ted and Alice* (1969), the story of a mate-swapping pair of couples, which was very successful and shot Gould to prominence. Wrote the Toronto *Globe and Mail,* "The performers achieve a marvelous improvisational quality; while they're all good at it, it's

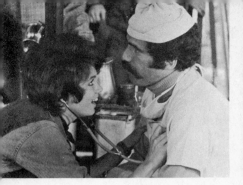

With Jo Ann Pflug in M*A*S*H
(1970)

In California Split *(1974)*

Elliot Gould who walks away with the movie, coming into his own as a light comedian."

*M*A*S*H* (1970) followed. It was one of the top grossers in Hollywood history, and Gould's film stardom became assured. He played Trapper John, the irreverent army surgeon who constantly undermines the military establishment in Korea. The film was rich in sick humor (SURGEON SEWING UP A PATIENT: "Is this an officer or an enlisted man?" NURSE: "Enlisted man." SURGEON: "Use big stitches.") and won first prize at the Cannes Film Festival. 20th Century-Fox, the production company of *M*A*S*H*, almost gained solvency with this entry, which also spawned a successful television series.

Gould's follow-up to his triumph was *Getting Straight* (1970), the story of a young graduate student alienated both from the college establishment and the campus activists. There were two more films in 1970 for Gould; both were flops. *Move* at least gave him a charming leading lady in Paula Prentiss; *I Love My Wife* offered him nothing. Nevertheless, the National Association of Theater Owners confirmed what Hollywood already knew: Gould was named the male star of the year.

In 1971, Gould appeared in the film version of his stage credit *Little Murders*. The satire, directed by Alan Arkin, was indeed rugged—some moviegoers walked out—but its power could not be denied. The leading role of an offbeat photographer who becomes catatonic when his wife is senselessly murdered fitted Gould like the proverbial glove.

Gould received an unusual honor when Ingmar Bergman chose him to star in *The Touch* (1971). He was the first American film actor to be directed by the famed Scandinavian artist.

Many felt that Gould was being endangered by overexposure at this juncture. Perhaps the strain of being a continual success was telling on him. His next project, *A Glimpse of Tiger,* had to be shut down due to personal difficulties (including troubles with costar Kim Darby and the director). He chose to take an extended vacation before tackling another project, and Hollywood observers suggested that his career was on the skids. Meantime Gould, who had taken to a carefree Hollywood existence, became allied romantically with actress Jennifer Bogart. They had two children and were eventually wed in 1974 but separated soon thereafter.

Director Robert Altman gave Gould his "comeback" role in *The Long Goodbye* (1973), an offbeat detective caper in which he portrayed a variant of the Philip Marlowe character. Also for Altman, Gould joined with George Segal in *California Split,* a study of gambling, and made an unimpressive would-be successor to *M*A*S*H* entitled *S*P*I*E*S* (1974) with Donald Sutherland.

Gould lives in Greenwich Village. He is an enthusiastic sports fan and a great admirer of psychoanalysis. His behavior is unpredictable. At the 1974 Tony Awards show, he presented an award to the musical *Gigi.* When no one came forth to claim it, Gould's mouth fell open, his face took on that famous vacant look, and the curly-haired star trotted off the stage without a word.

Films

1966: The Confession. *1968:* The Night They Raided Minsky's. *1969:* Bob and Carol and Ted and Alice. *1970:* M*A*S*H, Getting Straight, Move, I Love My Wife. *1971:* Little Murders, The Touch. *1973:* The Long Goodbye. *1974:* Busting, California Split, S*P*I*E*S. *1975:* Nashville,* Whiffs.

* Unbilled cameo

10. CARY GRANT

(ALEXANDER ARCHIBALD LEACH)

Born Bristol, England, January 18, 1904. Married (1) Virginia Cherrill, 1933 (divorced, 1935); (2) Barbara Hutton, 1942 (divorced, 1945); (3) Betsy Drake, 1949 (divorced, 1962); (4) Dyan Cannon, 1965 (divorced, 1968), child Jennifer. Height 6'1"; weight 175 lb; black hair, dark eyes. Sign: Capricorn.

Cary Grant is almost a synonym for *debonair*. Tall, charismatic, ever youthful, he is one of the great names of Hollywood. He is the type of star who is not being replaced by the new breed of performers.

Born in Bristol, England, Grant began life with the unfortunate name of Alexander Archibald Leach. The product of a broken home, he received a minimum of formal education. As a teen-ager he became a page boy at the British Hippodrome Theatre. Later

With Ingrid Bergman in Indiscreet *(1958)*

With Rita Hayworth and Jean
Arthur in Only Angels Have Wings
(1939)

With Ethel Barrymore in None But
the Lonely Heart (1944)

he joined an acrobatic troupe, working as a singer, dancer, and juggler. When the troupe went to America, the sixteen-year-old boy came along.

In 1923, Grant returned to England, but Arthur Hammerstein took note of him there and sent him back to New York to perform in Oscar Hammerstein's musical *Golden Dawn*. This led to roles on Broadway in *Polly, Boom Boom,* and *Nikki*. When the last closed, Grant went to Hollywood, won a contract with Paramount, and made his screen debut in *This Is the Night* (1932).

The suave Englishman quickly became a favorite through plenty of screen exposure in Paramount features. He appeared with Marlene Dietrich in bizarrely erotic *Blonde Venus* (1932) and starred opposite Sylvia Sidney in *Madame Butterfly* (1932). It was Grant to whom Mae West purred, "Come up 'n see me sometime" in *She Done Him Wrong* (1933). West also vamped Grant in *I'm No Angel* (1933). One unusual Grant role of this period was as the mock turtle in Paramount's all-star production of *Alice in Wonderland* (1933).

By 1936, Grant was so popular that it was not necessary for him to sign up again with Paramount, and he did not. It was a wise decision, as he went on to make joint arrangements with RKO and Columbia. *Topper* (1937) at MGM, cast him and Constance Bennett as stylishly witty ghosts; *The Awful Truth* (1937) paired him with Irene Dunne in a popular screwball farce; and he did two frothy comedies with Katharine Hepburn, *Bringing Up Baby* (1938) and *Holiday* (1938). *Gunga Din* (1939), an adventure yarn based on Kipling's poem, placed Grant in a different sort of role as a Cockney soldier; his performance was well liked, but sophisticated comedy would remain his forte.

During the forties, Grant continued as a top attraction. *The*

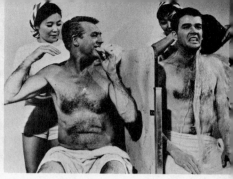

With Eva Marie Saint in North by Northwest *(1959)*

With Jim Hutton in Walk, Don't Run *(1966)*

Philadelphia Story (1940) had him as one of a triumvirate with Katharine Hepburn and James Stewart. *His Girl Friday* (1940) was a reworking of *The Front Page* that cast him as an editor and Rosalind Russell as his reporter ex-wife. One of Grant's most memorable performances was in the classic black comedy *Arsenic and Old Lace* (1944), in which he piled double take upon double take.

Grant was too old to serve in the armed forces during World War II, but on a number of occasions, he contributed the hefty salary he received for a film directly to the British war-relief cause.

Grant gave good straight performances at this time in two Hitchcock films, *Suspicion* (1941), in which Joan Fontaine feared he would do her in, and *Notorious* (1946) with Ingrid Bergman. In 1944, he won an Oscar nomination for *None but the Lonely Heart,* a story about some disreputable characters in wartime England. But it was comedy at which Grant excelled, be it with Loretta Young in *The Bishop's Wife* (1947), with Myrna Loy in *Mr. Blandings Builds His Dream House* (1948), or with Ann Sheridan in *I Was a Male War Bride* (1949). The last film was particularly funny, calling for Grant to dress in "drag" as a WAC, and it was one of the year's top-grossing movies.

By 1950, Cary was able to demand and receive $300,000 per picture. He was still plying his talents in a variety of genres. There was *Monkey Business* (1952), a wild comedy in which Marilyn Monroe was featured, and *The Pride and the Passion* (1957), in which Grant, Sophia Loren, and Frank Sinatra were upstaged in every reel by a gargantuan cannon. Alfred Hitchcock, who retained Grant as one of his favorite heroes, starred him with Grace Kelly in *To Catch a Thief* (1955) and with Eva Marie Saint in

North by Northwest (1959). Unfortunately, Grant refused two very popular 1950s films—*Sabrina,* in which his intended role went to Humphrey Bogart, and *A Star Is Born,* in which his role passed on to Bogart, who in turn relinquished it to James Mason.

By 1960, Cary's hair was graying, the clean-cut profile was beginning to sag, and the slender figure was beginning to fill out. Nobody seemed to notice, however, when Grant charmed Doris Day in *That Touch of Mink* (1962), one of the more popular sex comedies of the insinuating sixties. Even more successful was *Charade* (1963), in which Cary won Audrey Hepburn after a series of confrontations with villains James Coburn, George Kennedy, and Walter Matthau. Audiences adored dialogue like the following exchange:

HEPBURN: I'm so hungry I could eat a horse.
GRANT: I think that's what you ordered.

However, Grant's follow-ups were not so felicitous. *Father Goose* (1964) was a nothing entry despite Leslie Caron's presence, and *Walk, Don't Run* (1966) seemed to be constructed around the mere fact that Grant looked great for a man of sixty-two. It was his last film to date.

In 1970, Grant was awarded an honorary Oscar for his years of "brilliance" as a screen performer. (Illustrative of his ever-attractive appeal, the week of the ceremony saw him the defendant in a paternity suit.)

Grant has been married four times, once to an heiress (Barbara Hutton) and three times to actresses (Virginia Cherrill, Betsy Drake, and Dyan Cannon). His divorce from Cannon in 1968 proved particularly messy; among other accusations, she claimed that he used LSD. The now-divorced couple still have legal battles over their child Jennifer.

Is Grant's career over? Says the white-haired, bespectacled Cary, "I'm not really making pictures and I don't know whether I'll ever make any—or whether I'll make one or ten."

Films

1932: This Is the Night, Sinners in the Sun, Merrily We Go to Hell, Devil and the Deep, Blonde Venus, Hot Saturday, Madame Butterfly. *1933:* She Done Him Wrong, The Woman Accused, The Eagle and the Hawk, Gambling Ship, I'm No Angel, Alice in Wonderland. *1934:* Thirty-Day Princess, Born to Be Bad, Kiss and

Make Up, Ladies Should Listen, Enter Madame. *1935:* Wings in the Dark, The Last Outpost. *1936:* Sylvia Scarlett, Big Brown Eyes, Suzy, Wedding Present, The Amazing Quest of Ernest Bliss. *1937:* When You're in Love, The Toast of New York, Topper, The Awful Truth. *1938:* Bringing Up Baby, Holiday. *1939:* Gunga Din, Only Angels Have Wings, In Name Only. *1940:* His Girl Friday, My Favorite Wife, The Howards of Virginia, The Philadelphia Story. *1941:* Penny Serenade, Suspicion. *1942:* The Talk of the Town, Once upon a Honeymoon. *1943:* Mr. Lucky. *1944:* Destination Tokyo, Once upon a Time, Arsenic and Old Lace, None but the Lonely Heart. *1946:* Night and Day, Notorious. *1947:* The Bachelor and the Bobby-Soxer, The Bishop's Wife. *1948:* Mr. Blandings Builds His Dream House, Every Girl Should Be Married. *1949:* I Was a Male War Bride. *1950:* Crisis. *1951:* People Will Talk. *1952:* Room for One More, Monkey Business. *1953:* Dream Wife. *1955:* To Catch a Thief. *1957:* The Pride and the Passion, An Affair to Remember, Kiss Them for Me. *1958:* Indiscreet, Houseboat. *1959:* North by Northwest, Operation Petticoat. *1960:* The Grass Is Greener. *1962:* That Touch of Mink. *1963:* Charade. *1964:* Father Goose. *1966:* Walk, Don't Run.

11. DUSTIN HOFFMAN

Born Los Angeles, California, August 8, 1937. Educated Santa Monica City College, Pasadena Playhouse. Married Anne Byrne, 1969, child Jenna. Height 5'6½"; weight 135 lb; dark brown hair, dark brown eyes. Sign: Leo.

Dustin Hoffman doesn't look very much like an actor and certainly not like the typical movie star that once graced the golden age of Hollywood. Diminutive and particularly unhandsome, he is probably the least physically impressive of the seventies crop of superstars. He is, however, among the most versatile and the most talented of the bunch—and certainly one of the most in demand.

Life began for Hoffman in Los Angeles; his father built furniture, and his mother loved movies (she named her son after silent screen star Dustin Farnum). Musically inclined, Dustin majored in music at Santa Monica City College before heeding a desire for

In Little Big Man *(1971)*

dramatic training and switching to the Pasadena Playhouse. After some training, he set out for New York to crash the theater.

There was a considerable period of struggle, which Hoffman filled with jobs as a janitor and mental-ward attendant. Eventually some television and summer-stock work came his way, but it seemed to lead nowhere. Hoffman began to teach acting for a steady income. However, when stage opportunities off Broadway became available, he promptly left teaching and worked with Jon Voight (his future *Midnight Cowboy* costar) in a revival of *A View from the Bridge*. In his next play, *Harry Noon and Night* (1964), the young actor revealed his versatility by playing a hunchbacked German homosexual. When he subsequently portrayed an aging Russian misanthrope in *Journey of the Fifth Horse*, his abilities won him the Best Off-Broadway Actor Award.

A chance to become a Broadway name evolved in 1965 when Hoffman was chosen to replace Martin Sheen in *The Subject Was Roses*. Unfortunately, he burned his hands in a costly accident that kept him out of the show. So he returned to off-Broadway theater and a part in the British farce *Eh?* directed by Alan Arkin. Mike Nichols, who was then preparing to film *The Graduate,* saw a performance and thought Hoffman would be ideal for this picture's title role. (Hoffman had meanwhile appeared in an Italian-made quickie, *Madigan's Millions* (1966), with Cesar Romero.)

The result was a box-office smash hit, and *The Graduate* provided Hoffman with instant superstardom. As a fresh-out-of-college young man who spends his first free summer making love to the attractive, sexually aggressive wife (Anne Bancroft) of his father's business partner, Hoffman was just right. The *Saturday Review* called him "the most delightful film hero of our generation."

Numerous film offers came to Hoffman following this success, but all of them required a reprise of his *Graduate* character. He wanted no part of typecasting. In his words, "I could see my obituary: Dustin Hoffman died today. His first film, *The Graduate,* was a hit." As a result, he spurned the movies and made his Broadway bow starring in *Jimmy Shine.* The show received lukewarm notices, but Hoffman's presence kept the play running for a respectable length of time.

As his follow-up to *The Graduate,* he picked an offbeat role in an offbeat film: Ratso Rizzo, the pathetic crippled bum who tries to market Jon Voight's sexual services in *Midnight Cowboy* (1969). The film was a sordid parade of various perversities, somehow

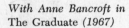

With Anne Bancroft in
The Graduate *(1967)*

With Mia Farrow in John and
Mary *(1970)*

effective enough to reap critical and popular huzzahs. Hoffman
explained his movie choice as follows, "I mean, he [Ratso] was so
sad, so grotesque, so loathsome. Ratso . . . there is so much you
can do with a part like that." Again his acting was extravagantly
praised. Both Voight and Hoffman were nominated for Best Actor
Oscars, losing out to John Wayne for his *True Grit* performance.

None of Hoffman's subsequent films has been as popular as his
first two starring assignments. *John and Mary* (1970), with Mia
Farrow, tried to blend the two stars with a lightweight tale of the
new morality that managed to please some moviegoers. Hoffman
then joined the ambitious *Little Big Man* (1971), a story of the
mistreatment of the American Indian. Much publicity accompanied
his quite remarkable makeup as a one hundred-year-old Indian,
which made him resemble a feathered mummy. The film was well
received but somehow missed the laurels expected for it. This was
followed by a disaster, *Who Is Harry Kellerman and Why Is He
Saying Those Terrible Things about Me?* in which Hoffman played
an emotionally baffled pop-song writer.

Commercially, Hoffman's greatest success of recent vintage has
been *Straw Dogs* (1971), a lavishly violent film directed by gore
specialist Sam Peckinpah. The picture provided Hoffman with a
perfect role for his special talents, that of a mild-mannered mathe-
matician beleagured by a low-living wife and an animalistic gang
in rural England.

Now a big-money star, Hoffman has lately traveled to Italy to
play in *'Til Divorce Do You Part* (1972) for a gargantuan sum. The
1973 epic *Papillon* cast him as a bespectacled Frenchman doomed
to life (?) on Devil's Island. Physically, he never looked worse
than he did in this motion picture, with a gaping bald spot and
distorting lenses. However, his acting and that of costar Steve
McQueen could hardly be faulted. In late 1974, Hoffman, under

With Susan George in Straw Dogs
(1971)

In Lenny *(1974)*

the energetic direction of Bob Fosse, appeared in *Lenny,* a bio-
graphical feature of that late, great, caustic comedian, Lenny
Bruce. Hoffman could hardly be blamed for the picture's failure
to capture the essence of that controversial entertainer.

Back in the 1960s, Hoffman had assisted Ulu Grosbard with the
stage direction of *A View from the Bridge.* In 1974, he assumed
direction of the Broadway-bound *All Over Town,* written by Murray Schisgal (also the author of *Jimmy Shine*).

Residing in New York, Hoffman was married in 1969 to Anne
Byrne, who the following year gave birth to their daughter, Jenna.
Regarding show-business stardom, Hoffman has said, "This sud-
den stardom stuff completely knocks you out of perspective."
While psychiatric analysis has kept him level headed, a film-studio
executive recently quipped, "He may be an anti-star, but he sure
gets superstar privileges."

Films

1966: Madigan's Millions. *1967:* The Graduate. *1969:* Midnight
Cowboy. *1970:* John and Mary. *1971:* Little Big Man, Straw Dogs,
Who Is Harry Kellerman and Why Is He Saying Those Terrible
Things about Me? *1972:* 'Til Divorce Do You Part. *1973:* Papillon.
1974: Lenny. *1976:* All the President's Men.

12. ALAN LADD

(ALAN WALBRIDGE LADD)

Born Hot Springs, Arkansas, September 3, 1913. Educated North Hollywood High School. Married (1) Marjorie Jane Harrold, 1936 (divorced, 1941), child Alan Ladd, Jr.; (2) Sue Carol, 1942, children David, Alana. Served with USAF, 1942 to 1943; medical discharge. Height 5'4½"; weight 155 lb; blond hair, green eyes. Sign: Virgo. Died January 29, 1964.

Alan Ladd, the pint-sized tough with the granite face, was the son of an English public accountant. His father died when Alan was a child, his mother remarried, this time to a house painter. In 1921, the family moved to California, where after some lean days, Alan's stepfather obtained a job in Hollywood as a movie studio's painter.

As an adolescent, Ladd distinguished himself as a superb ath-

In Whispering Smith *(1948)*

lete. At North Hollywood High, he was a swimming and track champion, and he also excelled as a swimmer with the Hollywood Athletic Club, becoming the diving champion of the West Coast in 1932. He saw such physical distinction as something of a necessity; he was only 5'4½" tall and felt compelled to surmount his nickname, Tiny.

Meanwhile, the ambitious youngster took on a variety of jobs. Stints as a lifeguard, potato-chip delivery boy, gas-station attendant, and newspaper boy eventually led to a spot as an apprentice actor at Universal Pictures. The training program lasted only four months, but it broke the ice and got Ladd before the cameras. His first appearance was in a bit as a projectionist in *Once in a Lifetime* (1932). Scores of bits followed in films for Paramount, Columbia, and Republic in addition to advertising shorts, and between his film debut and his stardom, Ladd claimed that he ignominiously appeared in about one hundred features.

It was, however, a precarious living. At times Ladd had to work as a technician on a stage crew, a cash-register salesman, a newspaperman, and even a hot-dog hawker to keep alive in those depression days. In 1936, he married Majorie Jane Harrold, and in 1938 Alan Ladd, Jr., was born. About this time, Sue Carol, an ex-star of silent days turned agent, heard Ladd on a radio show and was so impressed that she persuaded him to enlist her services. The two began making the rounds in pursuit of screen stardom for Ladd.

Much-needed screen exposure and experience followed. Roles ranged from serials like *The Green Hornet*, to big-budgeted pictures like *Citizen Kane* (1941), to thrillers like *The Black Cat* (1941). Ladd's real break came through RKO's *Joan of Paris* (1942), in which he played a downed British pilot pursued by Nazis and had a meaty death scene.

Ladd shot to stardom in 1942 as Raven, the hired killer, in *This Gun for Hire*. Paramount billed him fourth, but Ladd made it *his* picture. The critics, unlike the public, did not warm up to the tight-lipped new star and never would. Of Ladd's death scene in Veronica Lake's lovely lap, *Variety* noted, "Better men have died with their heads in less pleasant places." But moviegoers found Ladd a sensational new attraction, and the readers of the popular British magazine *Picturegoer* voted him the Best Actor Gold Medal of 1942.

Paramount placed Ladd on the contract roster. In another tense

With Veronica Lake in Saigon
(1948)

In The Black Knight *(1954)*

mystery yarn, *The Glass Key* (1942), he was again tough as spikes
and again made screen love to sultry Veronica Lake. Before long
he was topping fellow studio stars like Ray Milland, Fred Mac-
Murray, and Brian Donlevy in popularity polls. Meanwhile Ladd
and his first wife divorced, and he wed Sue Carol, who as an
agent continued to guide his high-powered film career.

The forties saw a series of terse, cigarette-puffing, tough-fisted
Ladd characterizations in films like *Lucky Jordan* (1942), in
which he played a gangster pursued by *two* glamour girls (Helen
Walker and Marie, "the Body," McDonald); *And Now Tomorrow*
(1944), where he was a downbeat but dedicated doctor who
cured Loretta Young of deafness; *The Blue Dahlia* (1946), another popular mystery with Veronica Lake (although he disliked
working with her); *Two Years before the Mast* (1946), a big box-
office sea epic, and *The Great Gatsby* (1949), where he appeared
in the title role. During these peak years, he received $75,000 per
film; was elected man of the year by *Photoplay* in 1943; and lent
his guest-star presence to such vaudeville-sketch pictures as *Variety Girl* (1947), in which he sang, and *My Favorite Brunette*
(1947), a Bob Hope comedy.

Ladd's film career had just begun to skid into decline when
Shane (1953) once again made him a major screen figure. This
western, directed by George Stevens, became a classic, and his on-
camera rapport with little Brandon de Wilde revealed new facets
of the Ladd screen persona. The picture grossed $9 million and
catapulted Ladd back among the top ten box-office attractions.

A variety of adventure, action, and romantic pictures followed—
The McConnell Story (1955), *Hell on Frisco Bay* (1955), with
Edward G. Robinson, and *Boy on a Dolphin* (1957), with Sophia
Loren. Ladd remained a cinema star of sorts until his death but
never again matched his landmark performances in *This Gun for*

With Brandon de Wilde in Shane
(1953)

With Carroll Baker in
The Carpetbaggers (1964)

Hire and *Shane.* He entered film and television producing, and he appeared with his son David in a particularly good feature, *The Proud Rebel* (1958).

On January 29, 1964, at the age of fifty, Ladd was found dead in bed at his Palm Springs home. Death was attributed to a mixture of sedatives and alcohol. His last picture, *The Carpetbaggers,* was released some months later.

Never secure in his star position, Ladd was unfortunately pursued by an inferiority complex about his acting that may have hastened his premature death. His second wife, behind his career to the end, once observed, "Alan has a great sense of insecurity. Every picture, he thinks, will be his last. He can never believe he is where he is or understand how he got there."

Films

1932: Once in a Lifetime, No Man of Her Own, *1933:* Saturday's Millions. *1936:* Pigskin Parade. *1937:* Last Train from Madrid, Souls at Sea, Hold 'em Navy. *1938:* The Goldwyn Follies; Come on, Leathernecks; The Texans. *1939:* Rulers of the Sea, Beast of Berlin. *1940:* Light of Western Stars, Gangs of Chicago, In Old Missouri, The Green Hornet (serial), Her First Romance, The Howards of Virginia, Those Were the Days, Captain Caution, Wildcat Bus, Meet the Missus. *1941:* Great Guns, Citizen Kane, Cadet Girl, Petticoat Politics, The Black Cat, The Reluctant Dragon, Paper Bullets. *1942:* Joan of Paris, This Gun for Hire, The Glass Key, Lucky Jordan, Star Spangled Rhythm. *1943:* China. *1944:* And Now Tomorrow. *1945:* Salty O'Rourke, Duffy's Tavern. *1946:* The Blue Dahlia, O.S.S., Two Years before the Mast. *1947:* Calcutta, Variety Girl, Wild Harvest, My Favorite Brunette.* *1948:* Saigon, Beyond

* Unbilled cameo

Glory, Whispering Smith. *1949:* The Great Gatsby, Chicago Dead-line. *1950:* Captain Carey, U.S.A. *1951:* Branded, Appointment with Danger. *1952:* Red Mountain, The Iron Mistress. *1953:* Thunder in the East, Desert Legion, Shane, Botany Bay. *1954:* Paratrooper, Saskatchewan, Hell below Zero, The Black Knight, Drum Beat. *1955:* The McConnell Story, Hell on Frisco Bay. *1956:* Santiago, Cry in the Night (narrator). *1957:* The Big Land, Boy on a Dolphin. *1958:* The Deep Six, The Proud Rebel, The Badlanders. *1959:* The Man in the Net. *1960:* Guns of the Timberland, All the Young Men, One Foot in Hell. *1962:* Thirteen West Street. *1963:* The Duel of Champions. *1964:* The Carpetbaggers.

13. STEVE McQUEEN

Born March 24, 1930, Slater, Missouri. Educated New York Neighborhood Playhouse. Married (1) Neile Adams, 1956 (divorced, 1972), children Terry, Chadwick; (2) Ali MacGraw, 1973. Served U.S. Marine Corps. Height 5'10"; weight 180 lb; blond hair, blue eyes. Sign: Aries.

Anyone who watched Steve McQueen play a bland second fiddle to the Blob in 1958 could never have foreseen where he would be in 1975. One of the highest-paid, most-idolized stars in movies, McQueen surmounted an unmemorable early career to become one of the current cinema's most genuinely exciting stars.

McQueen is elusive, and personal data hardly flows from him, but it appears that he was born in 1930 in Slater, Missouri. He was abandoned as a baby by his father and grew up principally in a reform school in Chino, California. After being released, the teenager worked as a merchant seaman, a lumberjack, and a carnival

With Tuesday Weld in The Cincinnati Kid *(1965)*

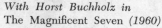

With Horst Buchholz in
The Magnificent Seven *(1960)*

In The Great Escape *(1963)*

barker, eventually joining the marine corps.

Following his service stint, McQueen arrived in New York, jumping from jobs like docker and bartender to positions as salesman or numbers runner. The fact that these jobs left a great deal to be desired did not bother McQueen; when everything became too tepid, he would head south and beachcomb in Miami. It was while laboring as a television repairman that he heard of the New York Neighborhood Playhouse, the dramatics school run by Uta Hagen and Herbert Berghof. McQueen was intrigued by the idea of an actor's life and entered the training program there in 1952.

The first professional experience for McQueen was in stock with Margaret O'Brien in *Peg o' My Heart.* Although his acting was quite dreadful, his intensity drew notice, and he soon appeared on Broadway in *The Gap.* His big New York break came in 1956 when he replaced Ben Gazarra as the dope-addicted Korean War veteran in the Broadway hit *A Hatful of Rain.*

McQueen's film debut was in *Somebody Up There Likes Me* (1956), a biography of Rocky Graziano; he performed little more than a bit. He followed this with *Never Love a Stranger* (1958), supporting John Barrymore, Jr. Then he landed the leading (human) role in *The Blob* (1958), the famous gooey science-fiction film. McQueen was the teenager who, parked with his girl friend one evening, first sees the Blob land on earth. (He was billed in these films as Stephen McQueen.)

At this point "Steve" McQueen tried television and became the star of the western series, "Wanted: Dead or Alive," beginning in 1958. The program was very popular until the star insisted that the stories needed more refinement, and much of the wallop was thus drained. However, mercurial McQueen was not upset; he was bored with the show and knew he could now have a lucrative movie career.

In Bullitt *(1968)*

With Ali MacGraw in
The Getaway *(1972)*

While still in the television series, McQueen had appeared in
the all-star *Never So Few* (1959), *The Great St. Louis Bank Robbery* (1959), and, most impressive, *The Magnificent Seven* (1960),
in which he was second-in-command of the famed pack of gun-
slingers (Yul Brynner, Charles Bronson, Eli Wallach, Robert
Vaughn, and so on). There followed *The Honeymoon Machine*
(1961), a pleasant enough comedy with Paula Prentiss; *Hell Is
for Heroes* (1961), a war thriller that costarred him with the
then red-hot Bobby Darin; and *The War Lover* (1962), a British
film with Steve as a World War II pilot.

McQueen's popularity and critical acclaim received a big boost
from the thriller, *The Great Escape* (1963). As Cooler King, so
dubbed because of his frequent prison banishments, McQueen
found a perfect role for his tough, driving, yet totally cool personality. The episode in which he eludes the Nazi pursuers on a
motorcycle that won't quit (he did his own amazing stunts) drew
cheers from audiences wherever it played.

During his struggling New York days, McQueen had married
Neile Adams, an actress who was in *The Pajama Game* when her
husband was in *A Hatful of Rain.* They had two children.

A string of good films followed. In *Love with the Proper
Stranger* (1963), the stranger was McQueen and the girl was
Natalie Wood. *Soldier in the Rain* (1963) costarred him with
Jackie Gleason, and the equally interesting *Baby, the Rain Must
Fall* (1965) found Lee Remick as his leading lady. One of his
sturdiest roles to date came in *The Cincinnati Kid* (1965), in which
he starred as a roving cardshark and had an outstanding supporting cast, including Edward G. Robinson, Joan Blondell, Rip Torn,
and enticing Ann-Margret.

There have been no real slumps for McQueen as he continues
to turn up in commercial screen assignments, whether on a

revenge mission as in the western *Nevada Smith* (1966) or in the midst of intrigue as in *The Thomas Crown Affair* (1968). *Bullitt* (1968) was a slick detective yarn set in San Francisco with an unforgettable chase scene. *Le Mans* (1971) revealed McQueen's well-publicized racing-car finesse in exciting style.

Many were amazed at McQueen's solid acting in *Papillon* (1973) as an indestructible denizen of Devil's Island. He ages to an interesting old character who finally manages to escape from the notorious penal colony where he has been tortured and betrayed reel after reel in this exciting if overlong feature. An expected Oscar nomination did not materialize.

The columnists have been in their glory of late over the breakup of McQueen's marriage to Neile and his subsequent affair with and marriage to actress Ali MacGraw. MacGraw left her husband, Robert Evans (head of Paramount studios), to be with Steve, her costar in Sam Peckinpah's *The Getaway* (1972), a hugely successful gangster caper. Now the McQueen-MacGraw union has splintered.

Now as before, McQueen stays removed from most of the Hollywood social scene. He still enjoys racing cars and motorcycles and still derives pleasure from performing on screen. He explains, "Acting is like racing. You need the same absolute concentration. You have to reach inside you and bring forth a lot of broken glass. That's painful."

Films

1956: Somebody Up There Likes Me. *1958:* Never Love a Stranger, The Blob. *1959:* Never So Few, The Great St. Louis Bank Robbery. *1960:* The Magnificent Seven. *1961:* The Honeymoon Machine, Hell Is for Heroes. *1962:* The War Lover. *1963:* The Great Escape, Love with the Proper Stranger, Soldier in the Rain. *1965:* Baby, the Rain Must Fall; The Cincinnati Kid. *1966:* Nevada Smith, The Sand Pebbles. *1968:* The Thomas Crown Affair, Bullitt. *1970:* The Reivers. *1971:* Le Mans. *1972:* Junior Bonner, The Getaway. *1973:* Papillon. *1974:* The Towering Inferno.

14. PAUL NEWMAN

Born January 26, 1925, Cleveland, Ohio. Educated Shaker Heights High School, Ohio; Kenyon College, Ohio; Yale University. Married (1) Jacqueline Witte, 1947 (divorced, 1956), children Scott, Susan, Stephanie; (2) Joanne Woodward, 1958, children Elinor, Tessie, Claire. Served U.S. Navy, 1944. Height 5'9"; weight 160 lb; light brown hair, blue eyes. Sign: Aquarius.

During the past decade, Paul Newman has traded on his blue-eyed good looks and effectively insolent manner to become one of the top draws in motion pictures. Recently his directorial work has made him a doubly impressive figure in the current world of cinema. More an antihero than a hero and more a personality than an actor, he symbolizes the movie star of the mid-twentieth century.

Born and raised in Cleveland, Ohio, Newman grew up with an

In The Life and Times of Judge Roy Bean *(1972)*

With Martin Balsam in Hombre
(1967)

With Claire Bloom in The Outrage
(1964)

interest in sports and originally chose a career in economics. After a stint in the Pacific as a navy radioman during World War II, he was active at Kenyon College on the football team and, more importantly, in theater. After ten college plays, he decided to become an actor.

Stock work in Wisconsin and Illinois followed. However, Newman's father died when he was just getting started, and he returned to Cleveland to operate the family sporting-goods firm. But acting still appealed to him, and in 1951, he turned the business over to his brother and entered Yale University to study drama.

Arriving in New York after his graduate study, Newman found work almost immediately in television drama and made his auspicious Broadway debut in *Picnic* (1953). The play won a Pulitzer Prize, and Newman won a contract with Warner Brothers. His first picture was the embarrassingly juvenile *The Silver Chalice* (1954), a religious epic; MGM subsequently borrowed him to star in *The Rack* (1956), in which he played a veteran of the Korean War on trial for collaborating with the enemy.

For a time, Newman divided his time between films and the theater. He played boxer Rocky Graziano in *Somebody Up There Likes Me* (1956), Billy the Kid in *The Left-Handed Gun* (1958), and won the 1958 best actor award at the Cannes Film Festival for his portrayal of Ben Quick in *The Long, Hot Summer*. This was Newman's best role to date. *Time* called him "as mean and keen as a cockle-eyed scythe." The film blended him with an excellent cast, including Joanne Woodward and Orson Welles. Claiming that "the theater is my true love," Newman crammed his schedule to appear on Broadway in successes like *The Desperate Hours* (1955) and *Sweet Bird of Youth* (1959), a Tennessee Williams drama that cast him as a decadent, blackmailing gigolo.

In Exodus (1960)

Newman was fortunate in landing some excellent Hollywood roles at this time. With Elizabeth Taylor and Burl Ives, he starred in *Cat on a Hot Tin Roof* (1958) as Buck, the ex-athlete with a broken leg and a drinking problem. *The Young Philadelphians* (1959) cast him as a power-hungry, impoverished young lawyer who plots his way to the top. He rose to success again, though less effectively, in *From the Terrace* (1960) and led an all-star cast as an Israeli resistance leader in Otto Preminger's road-show attraction, *Exodus* (1960). In 1962, he recreated his Broadway role in *Sweet Bird of Youth* with Geraldine Page again his costar. It was well done but overly scrubbed up for the movies.

There have been many successes for Newman in the cinema. His drifting pool shark of *The Hustler* (1961) and caddish cowboy of *Hud* (1963) reaped him Oscar nominations. Of *Hud* the *New York Times* said, "Paul Newman as Hud is tremendous—a potent, avaricious man, restless with all his crude ambitions, arrogant with his contempt, and churned up inside with all the meanness and misgivings of himself." *Harper* (1966) showed that Newman could effectively play a hard-nosed detective, and *Cool Hand Luke* (1967) demonstrated that he could ably portray the alienated individualist, here a chain-gang convict. The latter won him another Oscar nomination (he has not yet won an Oscar).

In 1947, Newman wed actress Jacqueline Witte, by whom he had three children. They divorced in 1956, and in 1958 he married screen performer Joanne Woodward, who frequently costars with her husband and who won a 1957 best actress Oscar for *The Three Faces of Eve*. They have three children.

As Newman has begun to age, he has let the physical change work for him. In the enormously successful *Butch Cassidy and the Sundance Kid* (1969), he played the over-the-hill Butch with

In Cat on a Hot Tin Roof *(1958)*

enough class to make his name a bigger draw than ever despite the competition from costar Robert Redford. In 1971, he starred with Woodward in *WUSA,* a poorly received attack on right-wing politics. Newman has always been politically active, campaigning for candidates on several occasions. *The Life and Times of Judge Roy Bean* (1972) once again offered him in the role of a familiar western figure.

In 1973, Paul reteamed with Robert Redford in one of the greatest box-office successes of the past decade, *The Sting.* While Newman was in his element as a crafty con artist, the picture really gave him little screen time and failed to earn the Oscar nomination for him that it provided for Redford. (Jack Lemmon won that year for *Save the Tiger.*) Nevertheless, *The Sting* won a best-picture Oscar, and Newman again benefitted from a box-office hit. Thereafter he was one of the many VIP stars to grace the "disaster" feature *The Towering Inferno* (1974).

Newman has also become a director. He so superbly directed his wife in *Rachel, Rachel* (1968), a study of loneliness, that he won the New York Film Critics award for best director, and in 1971, he took over the direction of his own vehicle, *Sometimes a Great Notion.* As director, and with Joanne Woodward again as the star, the Newmans created the screen version of the Pulitzer Prize-winning play *The Effect of Gamma Rays on Man-in-the-Moon Marigolds* (1972). Together with Sidney Poitier, Barbra Streisand, and others, Newman heads a production company called First Artists.

Still very active in politics, expounding most of the liberal causes, Newman lives with his family in California. For so successful and respected a member of the acting world, his opinion of his craft is curious: "It's silly, stupid, and nothing to do with being an adult."

Films

1954: The Silver Chalice. *1956:* The Rack, Somebody Up There Likes Me. *1957:* The Helen Morgan Story, Until They Sail. *1958:* The Left-Handed Gun; The Long, Hot Summer; Cat on a Hot Tin Roof, Rally 'round the Flag, Boys! *1959:* The Young Philadelphians. *1960:* From the Terrace, Exodus. *1961:* The Hustler, Paris Blues. *1962:* Sweet Bird of Youth, Hemingway's Adventures of a Young Man. *1963:* Hud, A New Kind of Love. *1964:* The Prize,

What a Way to Go! The Outrage. *1966:* Lady L, Harper, Torn
Curtain. *1967:* Hombre, Cool Hand Luke. *1968:* The Secret War
of Harry Frigg. *1969:* Winning, Butch Cassidy and the Sundance
Kid. *1970:* WUSA. *1971:* Sometimes a Great Notion. *1972:* Pocket
Money, The Life and Times of Judge Roy Bean. *1973:* The Mack-
intosh Man, The Sting. *1974:* The Towering Inferno. *1975:* The
Drowning Pool.

15. SIDNEY POITIER

Born Miami, Florida, February 20, 1924. Educated Governor's High School, Western Senior High School, Nassau. Married Juanita Hardy, 1950 (divorced, 1961), children Beverly, Pamela, Sheri. Academy award for best actor, 1963 (*Lilies of the Field*). Served with U.S. Army, 1942 to 1945. Height 6'2"; weight 185 lb; black hair, brown eyes. Sign: Pisces.

From the start of Sidney Poitier's screen career—with several successful forays into theater and television—his talent has promised to make him one of the foremost black actors of our time. Indeed, he became the first black superstar, at a salary of $750,000 per film plus percentage, and as such holds a special place in cinema history. For a long time, Hollywood used Poitier as a showcase for its integrating intentions, but he has always tried to sidestep the racial issue. He has his own array of priorities—first, as an American; second, as an actor; and third, as a black.

With Tony Curtis in The Defiant Ones *(1958)*

In Uptown Saturday Night *(1974)*

With Claudia McNeill in
A Raisin in the Sun *(1941)*

Poitier was born in Miami, Florida, the youngest of eight children of a Caribbean tomato farmer who brought his family to Florida during the annual vegetable-selling season. When he was three months old, the family moved to Cat Island in the Bahamas, where the boy grew up in an outdoor life. "I could climb trees as well as Tarzan himself," he said. Before he could complete school, he had to go to work to help his family. He encountered "frustration and confusion . . . tremendous loneliness" in segregated Miami and soon went north to New York. When the United States entered World War II, Poitier enlisted in the army, leaving a civilian life pockmarked by jobs as a bowling-alley pin boy, a public-toilet cleaner, and a dishwasher.

After his discharge in 1945, Poitier returned to humdrum New York living. Learning that the American Negro Theater was seeking actors, he offered his services, but his heavy Bahamian inflection kept him from landing a position. Not to be dissuaded, he bought a radio and listened to trained voices to improve his own then-faulty diction.

He applied again to, and this time was accepted by, the American Negro Theater, appearing in plays like *Days of Our Youth, Lysistrata,* and *Anna Lucasta.* This exposure led to his first film appearance in a 1949 army signal corps documentary called *From Whence Cometh Help.* There followed a stunning performance as a black doctor tormented by bigoted Richard Widmark in the excellent 20th Century-Fox *No Way Out* (1950).

It was not easy for a black performer to obtain substantial screen work. Poitier appeared in the English version of *Cry, the Beloved Country* (1952), joined the Harlem Globetrotters for *Go Man, Go!* (1954), and got a major break in *The Blackboard Jungle* (1955)

With Katharine Houghton in
Guess Who's Coming to Dinner?
(1967)

because although already 30, he looked youthful enough to play a delinquent high school student effectively. After appearing on television as John Cassavetes' understanding pal in *A Man Is Ten Feet Tall,* he repeated the role in the film version, *Edge of the City* (1957), winning an increasing amount of critical and public notice.

In the late 1950s, it seemed that each year brought Poitier at least one important film assignment. *Something of Value* (1957) cast him as a member of the dreaded African Mau Mau tribe. Then came Stanley Kramer's *The Defiant Ones* (1958), which presented Poitier and Tony Curtis as two escaping convicts shackled together by a four-foot piece of chain. For this performance, he won the Berlin Film Festival's Silver Bear Award as best actor of the year and was nominated, along with Curtis, for an Oscar (they lost to David Niven for *Separate Tables*).

Porgy and Bess (1959) followed, a "handsome, intelligent, and often gripping production" (*Variety*) and one in which the singing voices of the leads (Poitier, Dorothy Dandridge, and Diahann Carroll) were dubbed. More essential to Poitier's acting career was his stellar performance on Broadway in the sensitive black family drama *A Raisin in the Sun* (1959), a role that he recreated on screen in 1961. Also in 1961 came *Paris Blues,* a European-made feature in which he romanced (on and off screen) Diahann Carroll.

The turning point in Poitier's already amazing show business climb was *Lilies of the Fields* (1963). As a footloose and fancy-free ex-G.I. who "adopts" a quintet of bewildered Continental nuns in parched Arizona, Poitier won the Oscar that year. This honor made him the second black performer (Hattie McDaniel

With Mildred Joanne Smith in No Way Out *(1950)*

for *Gone With the Wind* was the first) to win an academy award.

After this triumph, Poitier appeared in a string of none-too-successful roles, including a Moor battling Vikings in *The Long Ships* (1964) and a cameo as Simon of Cyrene in *The Greatest Story Ever Told* (1965). Somewhat better were *A Patch of Blue* (1965), in which he aided blind girl Elizabeth Hartman; *The Slender Thread* (1965), in which he tried to talk Anne Bancroft out of suicide; and *To Sir with Love* (1967), in which he coped with hostile students and romantically inclined teachers.

There were two hits for Poitier in 1967. *In the Heat of the Night* cast him as a northern law-enforcement officer who shows bigoted southern police chief Rod Steiger a thing or two about homicide solving. (Steiger claims that Poitier's acting helped him win an Oscar for his own portrayal.) *Guess Who's Coming to Dinner?* (1967) was a financial bonanza that reunited Katharine Hepburn and Spencer Tracy on camera for the last time (Tracy died a few weeks after the film's completion). This story of interracial marriage was ridiculously simplified by Poitier's role as a clean-cut, highly educated, Nobel Prize-winning physician. (As radical H. Rap Brown said, "Even George Wallace would like that nigger.") Somehow, audiences did not seem to mind.

Since then Poitier has remained a familiar leading man on screen in films like *For Love of Ivy* (1969), *The Lost Man* (1969), *They Call Me MISTER Tibbs!* (1970) (a sequel to *In the Heat of the Night*), *The Organization* (1971) (another sequel), and *Brother John* (1970). A western, *Buck and the Preacher* (1972), found Poitier both starring and directing a film, a practice that he has continued in very recent years. His most popular feature lately has been *Uptown Saturday Night* (1974), which joined him with such names as Harry Belafonte, Flip Wilson, Bill Cosby, and Roscoe Lee Brown. In 1975, he appeared with Michael Caine in the London-produced film *The Wilby Conspiracy*, and directed and costarred in *Let's Do It Again*, the sequel to *Uptown Saturday Night*.

Divorced from his wife, by whom he has three daughters, Poitier lives well and privately. Columnists have enjoyed trying to trace his relationships with costars Diahann Carroll and Joanna Shimkus (by whom he has had two children) and writing up his lavish residences in the Bahamas and Manhattan. Resenting pressure groups that try to manipulate him into civil-rights efforts, he claims he wants to be accepted as just a human being. As far as his career is concerned, Poitier asserts, "You don't have to be very good to survive as an actor. You can get by on a number of things which don't add up to very much."

Films

1949: From Whence Cometh Help. *1950:* No Way Out. *1952:* Cry, the Beloved Country; Red Ball Express. *1954:* Go Man, Go! *1955:* The Blackboard Jungle. *1956:* Good-bye, My Lady. *1957:* Edge of the City, Something of Value, Band of Angels. *1958:* The Mark of the Hawk, The Defiant Ones. *1959:* Porgy and Bess. *1960:* Virgin Island, All the Young Men. *1961:* A Raisin in the Sun, Paris Blues. *1962:* Pressure Point, Lilies of the Field. *1964:* The Long Ships. *1965:* The Greatest Story Ever Told, The Bedford Incident, A Patch of Blue, The Slender Thread. *1966:* Duel at Diablo. *1967:* In the Heat of the Night, To Sir with Love, Guess Who's Coming to Dinner? *1968:* For Love of Ivy. *1969:* The Lost Man. *1970:* They Call Me MISTER Tibbs. *1971:* Brother John, The Organization. *1972:* Buck and the Preacher (also director). *1973:* A Warm December (also director). *1974:* Uptown Saturday Night (also director). *1975:* The Wilby Conspiracy. *1976:* Let's Do It Again (also director).

16. TYRONE POWER
(TYRONE EDMUND POWER)

Born Cincinnati, Ohio, May 5, 1914. Educated Sister of Mercy Academy, Preparatory School of the University of Dayton, Purcell High School, Cincinnati, Ohio. Married (1) Annabella, 1939 (divorced, 1948); (2) Linda Christian, 1949 (divorced, 1955), children Romina, Taryn; (3) Deborah Minardos, 1958, child Tyrone, born posthumously. Served with U.S. Marine Corps, 1942 to 1946. Height 6'; weight 170 lb; dark brown hair, brown eyes. Sign: Taurus. Died November 15, 1958 in Spain.

Few stars have had the looks, style, or genuine acting ability that characterized Tyrone Power. Blessed with a rich heritage of theatrical blood, Power was the great-grandson of the Tyrone Power who was a leading comic actor at the nineteenth-century London Drury Lane Theatre and the son of a Tyrone Power who was a famous stage actor in his own right. With such a background and

With Madeleine Carroll in Lloyds of London *(1937)*

In Blood and Sand *(1941)*

With Phil Carey in The Long Gray Line *(1955)*

such impressive looks from childhood, there was only one vocation ever really considered for Power.

After being educated in Catholic schools in his birthplace of Cincinnati, young Power accompanied his father to Hollywood in 1931. That December his father died on a sound stage in the arms of his seventeen-year-old son, and Tyrone moved with his mother and younger sister to Santa Barbara. Work in the community theater group there led to admission to Universal's apprentice workshop, where Alan Ladd was a classmate. Power flunked out almost immediately but not before he made his film debut in a featured role in *Tom Brown of Culver* (1932).

Power subsequently landed acting jobs in various places—a bit as a cadet in a Dick Powell-Ruby Keeler musical, *Flirtation Walk* (1934); radio and theater work in Chicago; stock in Massachusetts; and Shakespearean roles in New York with Katharine Cornell. At this juncture, 20th Century-Fox screen-tested him, liked what they saw, and signed him to a seven-year contract. *Lloyds of London* (1937), the story of the famous English insurance company, promptly boosted Power to stardom. "When sheer action and character delineation are concerned, he is excellent," reported the none-too-charitable *New York Times*, and an epic-film hero's career was born.

Fox saw Power originally as an answer to MGM's Robert Taylor, then the heartthrob of the silver screen. However, "Ty" (as his fans soon began calling him) quickly emerged with a style all his own. He promptly became the lot's most popular male star, romancing such box-office royalty as Alice Faye, Loretta Young, and Sonja Henie. Too often the flyweight scripts the studio assigned to him called for little more than allowing his smoldering good looks to fill as many close-ups as possible. Nevertheless,

With Gene Tierney in The Razor's
Edge (1946)

whenever a project came along that was to be given class-A production, the lead role went to Power.

In Old Chicago (1938) starred him, with Alice Faye and Don
Ameche, as the opportunist member of the O'Leary family whose
cow supposedly began the great Chicago fire. *Jesse James* (1939),
one of the all-time classic westerns, cast him as the ruthless and
attractive outlaw lead. In this role, Power was colorful and convincing, blazing his way from the farm boy victimized by the
oppressive railroad to the notorious outlaw murdered by an assas-
sin's bullet. *The Mark of Zorro* (1940) found him as the fabled
crusader of old California, fop by day and caped swashbuckler by
night. His climactic duel with evil Basil Rathbone is one of the
most exciting swordplays ever filmed. Power was even more exciting in *Blood and Sand* (1941). His performance as the tragic
matador earned him favorable comparison with Valentino, who
had played the role in the silent cinema. The film provided Power
with two gorgeous leading ladies, Linda Darnell and Rita Hayworth.

When the United States entered World War II, Power enlisted
in the marines, qualifying for officer's candidate school and eventually becoming a first lieutenant. As a pilot with the Marine Trans-
port Command, he was among the first to fly supplies to Iwo Jima
when the island was under enemy attack.

In 1946, Power returned to the Fox fold, starring with Gene
Tierney, Clifton Webb, and John Payne in *The Razor's Edge,* a
high-toned screen treatment of Somerset Maugham's enduring best
seller. Next came his best screen performance, as the famed mind
reader turned geek in *Nightmare Alley* (1947), a study of sleazy
carnival life, with Joan Blondell and Colleen Gray for distraction.
However, many of Power's fans were dismayed to see their war

Wth Jack Hawkins and Robert Blake in The Black Rose *(1950)*

hero as a down-and-out heel, and Fox ordered him back to dashing melodrama in *Captain from Castile* (1947). Thereafter Power
earned his paychecks at Fox playing in an eleventh-century Oriental drama (*The Black Rose,* 1950), some World War II rehash-
ings (*An American Guerrilla in the Philippines,* 1951), westerns
(*Rawhide,* 1951), and adventures (*King of the Khyber Rifles,*
1954). No longer receiving the star treatment (Gregory Peck was),
Power left Fox in 1955.

The remainder of his career was interesting and varied. There
was stage work (*John Brown's Body,* 1953; *The Devil's Disciple,*
1956; and *Mister Roberts,* 1950, in London; and an American tour
of *Back to Methuselah,* 1957), television (*Miss Julie* with Mai
Zetterling), and some excellent and popular films, notably John
Ford's *The Long Gray Line* (1955), in which Power was superb
as the long-time West Point athletic coach, Marty Maher. In *Witness for the Prosecution* (1957), directed by Billy Wilder, he completed a stellar acting triangle (with Marlene Dietrich and Charles
Laughton) as an aging roué who may or may not be the killer.
He also produced (as well as starred in) the English-made *Abandon Ship!* (1957), a grim study of lifeboat survivors.

On November 15, 1958, Power, in Spain making *Solomon and
Sheba* opposite Gina Lollobrigida, rehearsed a grueling duel scene
with long-time associate George Sanders. Feeling ill, he left the
sound stage and returned to his dressing room, where he suffered
a fatal heart attack. (Yul Brynner was rushed in to replace him
in the epic.) On November 21, he had a marine military funeral
at Hollywood Memorial Park Cemetery.

Power had married three times. In 1939 he wed French actress
Annabella; they were divorced in 1948. The following year he
married actress Linda Christian, by whom he had two daughters;
they divorced in 1955. The year of his death, he had married much
younger Deborah Minardos.

The handsome star once lamented, "I've done an awful lot of
stuff that's a monument to public patience." However, there was
much more acting potential behind his attractive profile than the
public ever had the opportunity to witness.

Films

1932: Tom Brown of Culver. *1934:* Flirtation Walk. *1936:* Girls'
Dormitory, Ladies in Love. *1937:* Lloyds of London, Love Is News,

Cafe Metropole, Thin Ice, Second Honeymoon. *1938:* In Old Chicago, Alexander's Ragtime Band, Marie Antoinette, Suez. *1939:* Jesse James, Rose of Washington Square, Second Fiddle, The Rains Came, Daytime Wife. *1940:* Johnny Apollo, Brigham Young —Frontiersman, The Return of Frank James, The Mark of Zorro. *1941:* Blood and Sand, A Yank in the RAF. *1942:* Son of Fury, This above All, The Black Swan. *1943:* Crash Dive. *1946:* The Razor's Edge. *1947:* Nightmare Alley, Captain from Castile. *1948:* Luck of the Irish, That Wonderful Urge. *1949:* Prince of Foxes. *1950:* The Black Rose, An American Guerrilla in the Philippines. *1951:* Rawhide, I'll Never Forget You. *1952:* Diplomatic Courier, Pony Soldier. *1953:* Mississippi Gambler, King of the Khyber Rifles. *1955:* The Long Gray Line, Untamed. *1956:* The Eddy Duchin Story. *1957:* Abandon Ship! The Rising of the Moon, The Sun Also Rises, Witness for the Prosecution.

17. ROBERT REDFORD

(CHARLES ROBERT REDFORD, JR.)

Born Santa Monica, California, August 18, 1937. Educated University of Colorado; Pratt Institute, Brooklyn; American Academy of Dramatic Arts, New York. Married Lola Jean Van Wagener, 1958, children, Shaune, David, Amy. Height 6′; weight 170 lb; reddish blond hair, blue eyes. Sign: Leo.

There are not many current stars to replace the greats who dominated the screen of the golden age. However, Robert Redford seems to be truly doing this. His handsome blond looks endear him to a vast following, and his acting is rarely faulted by even the most dyspeptic critic. Redford is one of the few movie names who can draw audiences to a film simply because he is in it.

Redford grew up in Santa Monica near the Hollywood studios. As a youngster, he joined in sports enthusiastically, raced hot-rod

With Robert Shaw and Paul Newman in The Sting (1973)

With Natalie Wood in Inside Daisy Clover *(1965)*

As The Great Waldo Pepper *(1975)*

cars, and every now and then broke into Bel Air mansions with his pals ("We never stole anything much; we just did it for kicks"). His adolescence found him just bumming around much of the time, but eventually he won a baseball scholarship to the University of Colorado.

Art had become a fascination of Redford's, and in 1957 he quit school, journeyed to Europe, lived in Florence and Paris, and painted. This bohemian way of life agreed with him, and upon his return to the United States, he enrolled at Brooklyn's Pratt Institute to study art. Simultaneously, he joined the American Academy of Dramatic Arts on the advice of friends, and he soon found acting even more aesthetically satisfying than painting. His experiences at the academy convinced him about an acting career ("I was suddenly so free I could do anything!").

On Broadway Redford gained parts of increasing size in plays like *Tall Story, The Highest Tree,* and *Sunday in New York.* He also developed his talents on such television shows as "Twilight Zone," "Alfred Hitchcock Presents," and "CBS Playhouse 90." On October 23, 1963, Robert achieved stardom on Broadway in Neil Simon's *Barefoot in the Park,* playing opposite Elizabeth Ashley. The play ran for four years, but Redford got bored and left after eight months. (He had been troublesome on stage toward the end of his engagement. "I created accidents and problems to break the monotony.")

Deciding that movies were more his medium, Redford appeared in four that turned out poorly: *Situation Hopeless—But Not Serious* (1965), based on a novel by Robert Shaw (who later costarred with Redford in *The Sting*); *The Chase* (1966), with Marlon Brando; and *This Property Is Condemned* (1966) and *Inside Daisy Clover* (1965), both with Natalie Wood.

With Mia Farrow in The Great
Gatsby *(1974)*

Finally in 1967, Redford was signed to recreate his *Barefoot in
the Park* role for the movies, with Jane Fonda as his costar. The
enormous popularity of this screen comedy made him a market-
able film personality. But everyone wanted him to repeat his *Barefoot* formula, and he balked. He encountered studio pressures and
even a lawsuit in his efforts to avoid typecasting, but he was glad
he did. In 1969, he scored a tremendous success as the bushy
mustached, laconic Sundance Kid in *Butch Cassidy and the Sundance Kid*. Paul Newman was Butch, and the pair complemented
each other perfectly in this story of bank robbers who find their
craft becoming tough and obsolete. The film became the highest-
grossing western of all time and made Redford an idolized star
who could pick and choose from an avalanche of offered scripts.

Redford coproduced his next picture, *Downhill Racer* (1969),
which dealt with the international competition of the skiing world.
Judged one of the best sports features ever made, it boosted Redford's stock even higher. However, his next movie, *Tell Them Willie
Boy Is Here* (1969) (he played a bigoted sheriff in pursuit of a
runaway Indian), bombed.

Another sports film, *Little Fauss and Big Halsy* (1970), cast
Redford opposite an unlikely costar, Michael J. Pollard, and did
not match the style of *Downhill Racer*. *Newsweek* reported, "Call
it a Redford movie. For Halsy is independent, lonely, running,
remote, obsessed—all the qualities we have come to expect from a
Redford hero." *Jeremiah Johnson* (1972) was an offbeat western in
which Redford played the rugged title role.

Much more winning at the box office was *The Sting, the* money-
making feature of 1973, in which Redford was again costarred
with Paul Newman. The plot, involving an elaborate hoax per-
petrated by Redford and Newman on villainous gambler Robert

With Jane Fonda in Barefoot in the Park *(1967)*

Shaw, enchanted audiences. The film won the best picture Oscar of 1973, and Redford was nominated for best actor, but he lost to Jack Lemmon of *Save the Tiger.*

Almost as successful was *The Way We Were* (1973), in which Redford and Barbra Streisand carried on a sad love affair spanning several celluloid decades. One of the great "crying" pictures of recent vintage, it was another box-office bonanza. To cash in on Redford's current drawing power, two of his earlier films, *The Hot Rock* (a heist caper) and *The Candidate* (about a California senatorial race), were reissued.

Paramount so loudly ballyhooed its remake of *The Great Gatsby* (1974) that it is unlikely that anything offered in this adaptation of the F. Scott Fitzgerald story could have lived up to expectations. Redford appeared as Jay Gatsby, the shady but idealistic hero, with Mia Farrow as Daisy, the object of his tremendous affection. Despite the film's failure to gain much critical or audience support, Redford's career continued at a rapid pace. Having completed *The Great Waldo Pepper* (1975), a film about a barnstorming pilot, he launched into *Three Days of the Condor* (1975), an account of secret activities within the CIA with Faye Dunaway as his costar. Next on his roster of assignments is a film version of the controversial nonfiction best-seller, *All the President's Men,* dealing with the Watergate scandal.

Since 1958 Redford has been married to Lola Jean Van Wagener, by whom he has three children. He divides his time between an Upper West Side Manhattan apartment and a mountain lodge in Utah. In his free time, such activities as skiing, horseback riding, and racing cars and motorcycles fill his schedule.

Redford does not claim that acting will remain his primary occupation. "I'll stay in acting until I get bored with myself or until I no longer enjoy it."

Hollywood does not enchant him; he refused to show up for the Oscar ceremonies in 1973, claiming to be busy with a film that was already completed. He seems not to care that his attitudes are not always well received, and this very private man refuses to take himself too seriously. His nickname for himself is "the Kid."

Films

1962: War Hunt. *1965:* Situation Hopeless—But Not Serious, Inside Daisy Clover. *1966:* The Chase, This Property Is Condemned.

1967: Barefoot in the Park. *1969:* Tell Them Willie Boy Is Here, Butch Cassidy and the Sundance Kid, Downhill Racer. *1970:* Little Fauss and Big Halsy. *1972:* The Hot Rock, The Candidate, Jeremiah Johnson. *1973:* The Way We Were, The Sting. *1974:* The Great Gatsby. *1975:* The Great Waldo Pepper, Three Days of the Condor. *1976:* All the President's Men.

18. BURT REYNOLDS

Born Waycross, Georgia, February 11, 1936. Educated Florida State College, Palm Beach Junior College. Married Judy Carne, 1963 (divorced, 1966). Height 5'11"; weight 175 lb; black hair, brown eyes. Sign: Aquarius.

No star currently enjoys as much wolf whistling and passionate fan mail from liberated women as does Burt Reynolds. After a decade of knocking around Hollywood playing half-breeds and heavies in television and forgettable movies, the slim, muscular, hairy-pelted actor has suddenly emerged as a major screen figure. The fame is well deserved—Reynolds has looks, he can act, and he has a personality that accepts his mammoth popularity with a large dose of humor.

Born in Waycross, Georgia, Reynolds was raised there and in Palm Beach, Florida, frequently sparking his adolescence with

With Sarah Miles in The Man Who Loved Cat Dancing *(1973)*

In Operation C.I.A. *(1965)*

With Angie Dickinson in
Sam Whiskey (*1969*)

run-away-from-home episodes. In high school, he dabbled in stage work but really excelled on the football team. As a result, he went to Florida State, quickly becoming an all-star Southern Conference halfback. However, a knee injury, aggravated by a car accident, sidelined him in his sophomore year, and before the school year was out, so was Burt.

Reynolds drifted to New York City, where to his disappointment jobs as a dishwasher and bouncer were all he could dredge up. Meeting some hopeful actors in Greenwich Village, he considered the stage and returned to study in Florida at the Palm Beach Junior College. Things clicked there, and in 1958 he won the Florida Drama Award, which led to a job at the Hyde Park Theater in New York City. There actress Joanne Woodward spotted the young actor and alerted an agent about his possibilities, and Reynolds's career began.

At the New York City Center, Reynolds played a sailor in a revival of *Mr. Roberts* that starred Charlton Heston. Shortly thereafter he made his television debut in an episode of "M Squad." Universal Studios took notice of his swarthy good looks (he somewhat resembled Marlon Brando) and acting talents and signed him to a seven-year television contract that was doomed from the start. The studio cast him in the series "Riverboat" in 1959. Reynolds and costar Darren McGavin feuded so much that Burt departed the weekly show before the end of the first season. While the evidence shows it was McGavin who was the unreasonable element of the fracas, it was Reynolds who was labeled temperamental. For a time work came infrequently; when it did, the call was usually for Reynolds to accent his part-Indian looks in menacing the leads in various television western series.

Reynolds became a regular on the "Gunsmoke" video series in

With Dom DeLuise in Fuzz *(1972)*   *In* Deliverance *(1972)*

1962, playing Quint Asper, a half-breed blacksmith. He had little to do on the program and left the show in 1965.

In 1966, he became the star of a new series, "Hawk," in which he portrayed a half-breed detective for the ABC television network. When the program was cancelled in mid season, the complaints were loud and clear. Thousands of angry letters to the network and an outcry from the press helped the show's star surmount a "flop" series.

Movies were no new medium to Reynolds; he had played in such duds as *Angel Baby* (1961) and *Armored Command* (1961). In his own words, "My movies were the kind they show in airplanes and prisons, because nobody can leave." However, now some good offers came his way. After doing the unspectacular *Navajo Joe* (1967), Reynolds starred with box-office charmer Raquel Welch and burly Jim Brown in *One Hundred Rifles* (1969), an affluent and popular western, and then starred in *Sam Whiskey* (1969) with leggy Angie Dickinson. Based on his success in these films, television reevaluated him. CBS cast him as Dan August, roughneck detective, in a series that ran out the 1970 to 1971 season. During this time, Reynolds began paying visits to the Johnny Carson "Tonight" show, where his wild sense of humor, high-pitched laugh, and curious charisma enormously boosted his popularity. He has revisited the show many times and occasionally guest hosts when the elusive Carson is absent.

In April 1972, Reynolds earned a strange niche in show-business annals when he became the first nude male fold-out for *Cosmopolitan.* "I thought it would be a kick," he explained. "It's intended as a put-down of *Playboy,* which I hate." The audience response was actually enthusiastic, and a large poster of the grinning, unabashed Burt was quickly marketed. While the publicity concerning the fold-out was at its peak, the film *Deliverance* was released. Reynold's performance therein as a rugged and stoical adventurer ("to survive—that's the game") won him enviable reviews.

Since then Reynolds has been maintaining stardom status in a steady flow of films. Woody Allen cast him in his wild spoof, *Everything You Always Wanted to Know about Sex but Were Afraid to Ask* (1972). Also in 1972 Reynolds starred in *Fuzz* in which at one point he disguises himself (mustache and all) as a nun and encounters Raquel Welch again. As the unorthodox private detective in *Shamus* (1973), he played opposite the enticing Dyan Cannon.

While shooting a western, *The Man Who Loved Cat Dancing* (1973), Reynolds was touched by scandal when an admirer of his costar, Sarah Miles, killed himself. If his detractors hoped this would handicap his career, they were wrong. *White Lightning* (1973), in which he played a cocky moonshiner, proved just as popular with the Reynolds fans as his previous vehicles. His *The Longest Yard* (1974), a prison drama, developed into one of the most popular films of the season.

Divorced from the comedienne Judy Carne (formerly of "Laugh-In"), and maintaining a steady relationship with the older Dinah Shore ("she's a great lady and we're having a lot of fun"), Reynolds divides his time between a home in Hollywood and 180-acre ranch in Jupiter, Florida, that was once a hideaway for gangster Al Capone. Reynolds, assisted by his dad, now raises Black Angus cattle there.

Currently, Reynolds is working on a series of late-night specials and can be seen in a theatrical film musical, *At Long Last Love* (1975), directed by Peter Bogdanovich. As for the snide comments doubting his effectiveness in a singing-dancing role, the star retorts, "I'm going to stick it in their ear!" (He has a powerful temper.)

Films

1961: Angel Baby, Armored Command. *1965:* Operation CIA. *1967:* Navajo Joe. *1968:* Shark, Impasse. *1969:* Sam Whiskey, One Hundred Rifles. *1970:* Skullduggery. *1972:* Fuzz, Deliverance, Shamus, Everything You Always Wanted to Know About Sex but Were Afraid to Ask. *1973:* The Man Who Loved Cat Dancing, White Lightning. *1974:* The Longest Yard. *1975:* W. W. and the Dixie Dancekings, At Long Last Love, Hustle.

19. GEORGE SEGAL

Born February 13, 1934, Long Island, New York. Educated Columbia University, B.A. 1955. Married Marion Sobel, 1958, children Elizabeth, Polly. Served U.S. Army, 1956 to 1957. Height 6'1"; weight 175 lb; brown hair, brown eyes. Sign: Aquarius.

Blessed with a marvelous flair for comedy and an impressive aptitude for drama, George Segal is definitely one of the most interesting stars of this generation. It's hard to believe that the boozed-up, mixed-up college teacher of the purging drama *Who's Afraid of Virginia Woolf?* is the same man who played the splendidly comic lawyer of the wicked farce *Where's Poppa?* Few actors have his range, and not many have the enthusiasm for acting that is so joyously evident in his work.

Segal is a native New Yorker, born in Long Island. His early education consisted of Quaker schools in Pennsylvania. During his

With Glenda Jackson in A Touch of Class *(1973)*

With Janice Rule in Invitation to a Gunfighter *(1964)*

With Elizabeth Taylor and Richard Burton in Who's Afraid of Virginia Woolf? *(1965)*

school days, he formed a jazz band, and after receiving a B.A. from Columbia University, he began seeking theater work.

He soon found it, but at first it was not as glorious as he had anticipated. At Manhattan's off-Broadway Circle in the Square Theater, he worked as a janitor, ticket taker, soft-drink salesman, and finally as understudy. Eventually he appeared with Peter Falk in Molière's *Don Juan.* It lasted one night. Segal started over again and had better luck in *The Iceman Cometh,* a production that also featured Jason Robards, Jr. This was an impressive credential, but the army chose an inopportune time to call, and Segal spent 1956-1957 in the armed forces.

After his discharge, Segal returned to New York City, appearing with the New York Shakespeare Festival in *Antony and Cleopatra* and *Leave It to Jane,* and sang in nightclubs with Patricia Scott. After playing in an off-Broadway revue, *The Promise,* Segal was drafted again—but this time by the movies.

His film debut was in *The Young Doctors* (1961). This was followed in 1962 by a half-minute bit in *The Longest Day*—and the decision to try television. Specials like *Death of a Salesman, Of Mice and Men,* and "The Desperate Hours," along with appearances in Broadway plays such as *Gideon* and *Rattle of a Simple Man,* returned Segal to films with a little more savvy on his part and a lot more respect on Hollywood's.

Act One (1963) about playwright Moss Hart, reunited Segal with off-Broadway associate Jason Robards, Jr., who played George S. Kaufman. The film flopped, but *Invitation to a Gunfighter* (1962) had put Segal in the midst of the excitement of an offbeat western that pitted Yul Brynner against the town boss, Pat Hingle. Another doctor chronicle, *The New Interns* (1964), followed before he obtained the title role of *King Rat* (1965), an effective, if down-

With Barbra Streisand in The Owl and the Pussycat (1970)

With Elliot Gould and Ann Prentiss in California Split (1974)

beat story about a Japanese POW camp in World War II. Segal in the conniving lead kept the film moving.

Following roles in the all-star *Ship of Fools* (1959) and *The Lost Command* (1966), Segal joined Richard Burton, Elizabeth Taylor, and Sandy Dennis in the controversial elaborate film version of Edward Albee's play *Who's Afraid of Virginia Woolf?* (1966). As Nick, the college history teacher used in bed by Taylor to torture her teacher husband (Burton) after a Saturday-night party, Segal won excellent notices, and he was nominated for an Oscar.

All kinds of formats followed for Segal including *The Quiller Memorandum* (1966), a spy caper; *The St. Valentine's Day Massacre* (1967), a gangster film; *The Girl Who Couldn't Say No* (1968), an Italian-made feature starring him opposite gorgeous Virna Lisi; and *The Southern Star* (1968), a film shot in Africa, where costar Orson Welles tried to devour the scenery. Segal was especially praised for his performance of the distraught husband-employee in *Loving* (1970), which costarred him with Eva Marie Saint.

In late 1970, two wild comedies were released that shone a new spotlight on Segal's ample comic talents. *The Owl and the Pussycat* was a big box-office film that cast him as a starving writer with Barbra Streisand as a starving hooker. Audiences roared at scenes like the one in which Barbra in a tacky negligee and George in a Halloween skeleton costume wrestle with a bottle of soda pop. Just as wild but not as commercial was *Where's Poppa?* a Carl Reiner concoction that was the height of slapstick. In this one, Segal was the unfortunate son of domineering, dangerously senile Ruth Gordon, who as one of her nasty habits insists on pouring Pepsi-Cola on her breakfast cereal.

Recently, semisuperstar Segal has been in such films as *The Hot*

Rock (1972), a heist caper; *A Touch of Class* (1973), a delightfully sophisticated comedy that won his costar Glenda Jackson an
Oscar; and *The Terminal Man* (1974), a modernistic story of
science gone wrong. He also appears on television—he starred in
the 1973 special "The Lie," had his own late-night special in late
1974, and frequently visits such talk-show hosts as Johnny Carson
and Merv Griffin, proving a perfect foil for his hosts' humor and
a lively guest at all times. He's still a passionate banjo player, and
he has recorded an album of ragtime tunes and banjo numbers
called *The Yama Yama Man*.

Segal's future in the show-business spheres appears unlimited.
Reflecting on his career and the cinema in general, he says, "I've
been party to everything I've done. I don't think you can go up
now and not be involved. There's no Big Daddy anymore—no
studios to take care of you, to say this script is for you. That was
a fascist dictatorship. . . . But we're all together now, and it's
producing more intelligent movies."

Films

1961: The Young Doctors. *1962:* The Longest Day, Invitation to
a Gunfighter, The Young Interns. *1963:* Act One. *1964:* The New
Interns. *1965:* King Rat, Ship of Fools. *1966:* The Lost Command,
Who's Afraid of Virginia Woolf? The Quiller Memorandum. *1967:*
The St. Valentine's Day Massacre. *1968:* The Girl Who Couldn't
Say No, The Southern Star, No Way to Treat a Lady, Bye Bye
Braverman. *1969:* The Bridge at Remagen. *1970:* The Owl and the
Pussycat, Loving, Where's Poppa? *1971:* Born to Win. *1972:* The
Hot Rock. *1973:* A Touch of Class, Blume in Love. *1974:* The
Terminal Man, California Split. *1975:* The Black Bird, Kosygin Is
Coming.

20. JAMES STEWART

(JAMES MAITLAND STEWART)

Born Indiana, Pennsylvania, May 20, 1908. Educated Mercersburg Academy, Pa., Princeton University. Married Gloria Hatrick McLean, 1949, children Ronald, Michael, Judy, Kelly. Academy award for best actor, 1940 (*The Philadelphia Story*). Served U.S. Army Air Force, 1941–1968, retired brigadier general. Height 6'3"; weight 167 lb; brown (now gray) hair, gray eyes. Sign: Gemini.

For 40 years, James Stewart has symbolized an Americana that somehow survives effectively in the cynical perspective of the 1970s. More personality than actor, he nevertheless has a performing credibility that has contributed to many film classics and has made several poor films more than tolerable.

Born in the small Pennsylvania town of Indiana, where his father owned a hardware store, Stewart grew up in a homey atmosphere

With Carole Lombard in Made for Each Other *(1939)*

With June Allyson in The Glenn
Miller Story (1954)

With Katharine Hepburn, John
Howard, and Mary Nash in
The Philadelphia Story (1940)

that remained a firm part of his character. At one time, he wanted
to become a naval academy plebe, but instead he opted for Princeton, graduating in 1932. Even though he majored in civil engineer-
ing and architecture, Stewart had little idea about a career, and
after graduation, he became an accordion player in a Massachusetts tea restaurant. This led to small roles with Joshua Logan's
University Players, a group including Henry Fonda, Kent Smith,
and Margaret Sullavan. The minor stage exposure convinced him
that he wanted to be an actor.

Stewart went to New York City and managed to land on Broadway in a succession of plays—Carry Nation, Goodbye Again,
Spring in Autumn, All Good Americans, Yellow Jack, Divided by
Three, Page Miss Glory, and Journey at Night. During this period,
an MGM talent scout took notice, and Stewart was signed to a
studio contract.

Metro was not sure, for a time, what to do with the twenty-
seven-year-old actor who was tall and gawky—hardly the physique
for a leading man. He made his debut as a reporter in Murder Man
(1935), followed by such roles as Jeanette MacDonald's outlaw
brother in Rose Marie (1936), a sailor who warbles two Cole
Porter tunes in Born to Dance (1936), a newspaper editor with a
padded suit and penciled mustache in The Last Gangster (1937),
and a football player in Navy Blue and Gold (1937). Stewart loves
to recall the time that the studio assigned him to a screen test for
an Oriental role in The Good Earth (1937). His stringbean appearance and small-town drawl made it one of the most disastrously
funny test reels ever filmed.

Stewart scored in a 1937 remake of Seventh Heaven (on loan to
Fox) and particularly in MGM's Of Human Hearts (1938). In this

In That's Entertainment *(1974)*

feature he portrayed an ambitious young man admonished by President Abe Lincoln when he neglects to write to his mother. On the strength of these performances, he became a new star in the Metro constellation.

In 1939, there were two top successes for Stewart, both on loan from MGM. *Mr. Smith Goes to Washington,* directed by Frank Capra at Columbia, provided him with one of his greatest roles, as the young, idealistic senator snared and exploited by crooked politicians. His olympian filibuster at the film's climax is unforgettable, and he was nominated for an Oscar. (Robert Donat of *Goodbye, Mr. Chips* won.) At Universal, Stewart was in *Destry Rides Again,* a raucous spoof of the western genre. The sultry Marlene Dietrich played opposite him as the provocative dancehall songbird called Frenchy.

With these credentials, Stewart was cast with Katharine Hepburn and Cary Grant in *The Philadelphia Story* (1940). The sophisticated comedy presented him as a reporter unimpressed by Hepburn's wealth (though very impressed by the lady herself). Again he was nominated for an Oscar, and this time he won (according to rumor because of being bypassed the year before for *Mr. Smith*). The trophy is on display at his father's hardware store in Pennsylvania.

When the United States entered World War II, Stewart, who had a commercial pilot's license, volunteered for air force duty. He was refused due to being underweight. Promptly beginning a diet that included lots of bread and bananas, he soon surmounted this problem and became one of Hollywood's most active participants in combat. He became a lieutenant colonel, commanded a B–24 squadron in England, flew twenty bombing missions over

With Almira Sessions (right) in Harvey (1950)

Germany, and won the Air Force Medal, the Croix de Guerre, and the Distinguished Fying Cross. (In 1959, he became a brigadier general.)

Coming back from the war, Stewart declined an invitation to return to MGM. He preferred to free-lance and became the first major star of the forties to work out a percentage-of-profits deal for his screen services. Among the excellent features in which he played at this time were Capra's irresistible fantasy, *It's a Wonderful Life* (1946); Alfred Hitchcock's thriller, *Rope* (1948); and *The Stratton Story* (1949), in which he played the Chicago White Sox pitcher who lost a leg. And, of course, there was *Harvey* (1950), in which Stewart played Elwood P. Dowd, the eccentric who might or might not have had a six-foot rabbit for a chum. Again he was nominated for an Oscar.

Long one of Hollywood's most notable bachelors, Stewart was finally wed in 1949 to ex-model Gloria Hatrick McLean. He gained two sons by her previous marriage and in 1951 became the father of twin girls, Judy and Kelly. (One stepson was killed in Vietnam.)

Over the years, Stewart has worked with some top directors in top pictures—Alfred Hitchcock starred him in *Rear Window* (1954), *The Man Who Knew Too Much* (1956), and *Vertigo* (1958); Otto Preminger recruited him to play the offbeat lawyer of *Anatomy of a Murder* (1959) (another Oscar nomination); Cecil B. De Mille cast him as a clown in *The Greatest Show on Earth* (1952); and John Ford enlisted him for *Two Rode Together* (1961), *The Man Who Shot Liberty Valance* (1962) (starring opposite John Wayne), and *Cheyenne Autumn* (1964). Such memorable pictures as *The Glenn Miller Story* (1954), *The Spirit of St. Louis* (1957) as Charles Lindbergh, *Bell, Book, and Candle* (1958), *How the West Was Won* (1963), and *Shenandoah* (1965) have also benefited from Stewart's ever-convincing presence.

Recently Stewart has divided his schedule between movies, the stage (he appeared on Broadway with Helen Hayes in *Harvey* in 1970, and repeated the role in London in 1975), and television (including two unsuccessful video series). When he makes a guest appearance on such programs as "The Dean Martin Show" and "Tonight," the audience's reaction is warmly enthusiastic.

Stewart recalls with pleasure the many leading ladies he has worked with (Jean Harlow, Joan Crawford, Claudette Colbert, Marlene Dietrich, Katharine Hepburn, Maureen O'Hara, and so on). He has seen an old Hollywood disappear and a new, less exciting one replace it. As he says with characteristic humor, "In the old days, when you went on location, they sent a limousine to your home to take you. Now they give you a map."

Films

1935: Murder Man. *1936:* Rose Marie, Next Time We Love, Wife vs. Secretary, Small Town Girl, Speed, The Gorgeous Hussy, Born to Dance, After the Thin Man. *1937:* Seventh Heaven, The Last Gangster, Navy Blue and Gold. *1938:* Of Human Hearts, Vivacious Lady, Shopworn Angel, You Can't Take It with You. *1939:* Made for Each Other, Ice Follies of 1939, It's a Wonderful World, Mr. Smith Goes to Washington, Destry Rides Again. *1940:* The Shop Around the Corner, The Mortal Storm, No Time for Comedy, The Philadelphia Story. *1941:* Come Live with Me, Pot o' Gold, Ziegfield Girl. *1946:* It's a Wonderful Life. *1947:* Magic Town. *1948:* Call Northside 777, On Our Merry Way, Rope, You Gotta Stay Happy. *1949:* The Stratton Story, Malaya. *1950:* Winchester '73, Broken Arrow, The Jackpot, Harvey. *1951:* No Highway in the Sky. *1952:* The Greatest Show on Earth, Bend of the River, Carbine Williams. *1953:* The Naked Spur, Thunder Bay. *1954:* The Glenn Miller Story, Rear Window. *1955:* The Far Country, Strategic Air Command, The Man from Laramie. *1956:* The Man Who Knew Too Much. *1957:* Night Passage, The Spirit of St. Louis. *1958:* Vertigo; Bell, Book, and Candle. *1959:* Anatomy of a Murder, The FBI Story. *1960:* The Mountain Road. *1961:* Two Rode Together, X–15 (narrator). *1962:* The Man Who Shot Liberty Valance, Mr. Hobbs Takes a Vacation. *1963:* How the West Was Won; Take Her, She's Mine. *1964:* Cheyenne Autumn. *1965:* Dear Brigitte, Shenandoah. *1966:* Flight of the Phoenix, The Rare Breed. *1968:* Firecreek, Bandolero! *1970:* The Cheyenne Social Club. *1971:* Fool's Parade. *1974:* That's Entertainment.

21. SPENCER TRACY

Born Milwaukee, Wisconsin, April 5, 1900. Educated Marquette Academy; Northwestern Military Academy; Ripon College, Wisconsin; American Academy of Dramatic Arts. Married Louise Treadwell, 1923 (separated), children John, Suzy. Academy awards for best actor, 1937 (*Captains Courageous*) and 1938 (*Boys Town*). Served with U.S. Navy, 1918. Height 5′10½″; weight 165 lb; dark brown hair, blue eyes. Sign: Aries. Died June 10, 1967.

Katharine Hepburn once said of her frequent costar Spencer Tracy, "He has an enormous integrity. He's like an old oak tree, or the summer, or the wind. He belongs to an era when men were men." Since Tracy's death in 1967, there has been no one quite like him, no one who can act so effectively yet so simply.

Born in Milwaukee, Tracy grew up in a tough neighborhood, became a tough kid, and gave his parents and teachers plenty of

With Lyle Talbot in Twenty Thousand Years in Sing Sing *(1933)*

With Irene Dunne in A Guy Named Joe *(1943)*

With Deborah Kerr in Edward, My Son *(1949)*

problems. At Ripon College, he was active in debating, which led to acting, which led to his leaving Ripon to study at the American Academy of Dramatic Arts. In 1918, Tracy, with Pat O'Brien, his neighbor and later costar and friend, enlisted in the navy during World War I, but he never left the United States. He was soon mustered out of the service as the war ended.

After graduating from the American Academy of Dramatic Arts in 1923, Tracy began a seven-year stint as a stage actor, doing extensive stock and appearing on Broadway in plays like *Yellow, Baby Cyclone,* and *The Last Mile.* In *The Last Mile,* he played a rough convict named Killer Mears and drew the attention of Hollywood.

Tracy's actual film debut was in some Vitaphone short subjects for Warner Brothers in their New York studio, but his first major role was in John Ford's *Up the River* (1930). Again his part was that of a prisoner. The Fox Corporation was sufficiently impressed with his screen presence to sign him to a long-term contract. In the next five years, Tracy appeared in over two dozen features for the studio. Only two of them were in any way memorable—*The Power and the Glory* (1933), in which he played a railroad tycoon; and *Twenty Thousand Years in Sing Sing* (1933), in which, on loan to Warner Brothers, he played yet another convict with Bette Davis as his costar.

In 1935, Tracy switched studios and joined the roster at MGM, where the right roles in the right pictures made him one of Metro's most popular stars. In *Fury* (1936), Fritz Lang's classic condemnation of mob violence, Tracy played a man hounded by vicious townspeople for a crime he did not commit. The film boosted his industry standing. *San Francisco* (1936), in which he costarred with Clark Gable and Jeanette MacDonald, cast him as a priest and got him his first of six Oscar nominations.

In It's a Mad, Mad, Mad, Mad
World *(1964)*

In 1937, Tracy won the Oscar for his moving portrayal of Manuel, the Portuguese fisherman in the splendid *Captains Courageous*. He had originally feared the role, with its songs and curly-headed make-up (Joan Crawford supposedly greeted him with, "Hey, it's Harpo Marx!"). However, he overcame his reluctance and offered what is perhaps his finest screen work. No longer under the shadow of the studio's kingpin, Clark Gable, he was now a personality of the first rank himself. In 1938, he won his second Oscar for *Boys Town,* becoming the first screen actor to receive two best actor awards and the first to receive an Oscar in two successive years.

With Gable, Spencer starred in *Test Pilot* (1938) and *Boom Town* (1940). He joined with one of MGM's most lustrous stars (and one of his favorite coworkers), Joan Crawford, in *Mannequin* (1938); was Hedy Lamarr's romantic interest in *I Take This Woman* (1940); and was provided with two enchanting coleads, Ingrid Bergman and Lana Turner, when he superbly played the title role(s) in *Dr. Jekyll and Mr. Hyde* (1941).

During his peak Hollywood years, Tracy was a moody man, never hobnobbing with the social set and on occasion difficult to handle. In 1923, he had married Louise Treadwell, an actress he met in stock. They had two children, a boy and a girl; the boy was born deaf, and Mrs. Tracy eventually founded the John Tracy Clinic at the University of Southern California to aid other deaf children. Tracy and his wife separated early in his film career, and despite off-and-on reconciliations and though he kept in touch with his family, there was never a permanent domestic peace.

In 1942, Tracy teamed with Katharine Hepburn in *Woman of the Year*. The result was a near perfect screen duo, the chemistry sparking such further vehicles for the contrasting stars as *Keeper of the Flame* (1943), *Without Love* (1945), *State of the Union*

With Katharine Hepburn in Woman of the Year *(1942)*

(1948), *Adam's Rib* (1949), *Pat and Mike* (1952), *The Desk Set* (1957), and *Guess Who's Coming to Dinner?* (1967). Off screen, Hepburn and Tracy began a relationship that was, if not openly and conventionally romantic, evidently very close.

Over the years, there were many professional triumphs for Tracy. His graying hair and added weight merely augmented his screen authority. *Father of the Bride* (1950) cast him as Elizabeth Taylor's dad in a delightful comedy; *Bad Day at Black Rock* (1955) starred him as a one-armed government agent battling the small-town prejudice of such heavies as Lee Marvin and Ernest Borgnine; *The Old Man and the Sea* (1958) found him as the stoical Cuban fisherman in the film version of Ernest Hemingway's classic tale; *The Last Hurrah* (1958) reunited him with director John Ford and cast him as a political boss; *Judgment at Nuremborg* (1961) saw him as a judge presiding over the Nazi war-crimes trials.

At Fox during the 1930s, Tracy had become a problem performer, often unpredictable because of his temperament and hard-drinking habits. In the 1950s, his dependability was problematic as he became more finicky with advancing age. In the 1960s, repeated illness from a heart condition caused him to drop out of one film project after another (often being replaced by his contemporary Edward G. Robinson). Another result of Tracy's ill health was that he became increasingly reclusive.

Although his condition was worsening, Tracy agreed to work with Katharine Hepburn again in a project directed by his friend Stanley Kramer. The film (which exploited the Sidney Poitier image) was *Guess Who's Coming to Dinner?* (1967), an unrealistic racial comedy. Production was a bit morbid, as Tracy's scenes were shot quickly in case the actor expired at an inopportune time. He made it, and the picture, released after Tracy's death, did great business as the public flocked to see one of their great favorites for the last time. The film gained him his sixth Oscar nomination.

When Tracy died of a heart attack, on June 10, 1967, he ended forty years in a profession he insisted he despised. He was unimpressed by his Oscars. "I couldn't care less whether I received an Oscar or not" he said. "Oscars don't mean a damn thing. More than award for ability, it's likely to be a sentimental award given you by your friends." And as for acting, he had this to say: "I really don't like acting. I don't like anything about it, you might

say. But I did very well from it. It's never been demanding. It
doesn't require much brainwork. Acting isn't the noblest profession in the world but there are things lower than acting. Not
many, mind you, but politicians give you something to look down
on from time to time. Don't ask me about acting. I don't know
what acting is."

Films

1930: Up the River. *1931:* Quick Millions, Six Cylinder Love.
1932: She Wanted a Millionaire, Sky Devils, Disorderly Conduct,
Young America, Society Girl, Painted Woman, Me and My Gal.
1933: Twenty Thousand Years in Sing Sing, Face in the Sky,
Shanghai Madness, The Power and the Glory, The Mad Game,
Man's Castle. *1934:* Looking for Trouble, The Show-Off, Bottoms
Up, Now I'll Tell, Marie Galante. *1935:* It's a Small World, Murder
Man, Dante's Inferno, Whipsaw, Riffraff. *1936:* Fury, San Fran-
cisco, Libeled Lady. *1937:* They Gave Him a Gun, Captains
Courageous, Big City. *1938:* Mannequin, Test Pilot, Boys Town.
1939: Stanley and Livingstone. *1940:* I Take This Woman, North-
west Passage, Edison the Man, Boom Town. *1941:* Men of Boys
Town, Dr. Jekyll and Mr. Hyde. *1942:* Woman of the Year, Tortilla
Flat, Keeper of the Flame. *1943:* A Guy Named Joe, The Seventh
Cross. *1944:* Thirty Seconds over Tokyo. *1945:* Without Love. *1947:*
The Sea of Grass, Cass Timberlane. *1948:* State of the Union. *1949:*
Edward, My Son; Adam's Rib. *1950:* Malaya, Father of the Bride.
1951: Father's Little Dividend, The People against O'Hara. *1952:*
Pat and Mike, Plymouth Adventure. *1953:* The Actress. *1954:*
Broken Lance, Bad Day at Black Rock. *1956:* The Mountain. *1957:*
Desk Set. *1958:* The Old Man and the Sea, The Last Hurrah. *1960:*
Inherit the Wind. *1961:* The Devil at Four o'Clock, Judgment at
Nuremberg. *1963:* It's a Mad, Mad, Mad, Mad World. *1967:* Guess
Who's Coming to Dinner?

22. JOHN WAYNE
(MARION MICHAEL MORRISON)

Born Winterset, Iowa, May 26, 1907. Educated Glendale High School, California; University of Southern California. Married (1) Josephine Saenz, 1933 (divorced, 1944), children Antonio, Melinda, Michael, Patrick; (2) Esperanza Baur, 1946 (divorced, 1953); (3) Pilar Pallette, 1954 (separated, 1973), children Aissa, Marisa, Ethan. Height 6'4"; weight 210 lb; brown hair, blue eyes. Sign: Gemini.

Superstars come and go in the motion-picture business, but John ("Duke") Wayne is indestructible, or so it would seem. As MGM's Louis B. Mayer once said, "John Wayne has an endless face, and he can go on forever." In 1975, it looks as though he'll do just that.

Born in Winterset, Iowa, where his father was a druggist, Wayne was christened Marion Michael Morrison. The Morrisons later moved to Glendale, California. Wayne performed in some of

With Marlene Dietrich in Seven Sinners *(1940)*

In True Grit *(1969)*   *With James Watkins in* McQ *(1974)*

the plays at Glendale High, was a star on the high-school football team, and sometimes after classes worked in his father's drugstore.

Wayne's earliest ambition was to become a naval officer; when an appointment to the naval academy failed to materialize, he settled for a berth on a freighter on route to Honolulu. It was unexciting enough to make him change his plans, and upon returning home, young Marion suffered through several odd jobs as iceman, truck driver, and fruit picker. Finally, a football scholarship to the University of Southern California saved him from such labors and started him in the right direction.

Meanwhile, he found work in the Fox prop department, where his husky 6′ 4″ frame brought him to the attention of the famous director John Ford. Ford took a liking to the lad and gave him bits in such features as *Mother Machree* (1928), *Hangman's House* (1928), and *Men without Women* (1930). Reportedly it was Ford who suggested him to Raoul Walsh for the male lead in *The Big Trail* (1930), a sweeping study of old Oregon filmed in a wide-screen process. At this time, his professional name was changed to John Wayne. (Walsh had advised the young man that Marion Michael Morrison "sounds like a circuit preacher.") For *The Big Trail*, Wayne's reviews were decent, but the film was a box-office dud.

Thereafter, Wayne began an eight-year run as one of Hollywood's busiest frequently pummeled heroes—of unspectacular movies. For such "poverty row" studios as Columbia and Monogram, he starred in a rash of "three-day wonders," quickies with the accent on fist fights and the production schedule on speed. He also starred in the Mascot pictures, serials like *Shadow of the Eagle* (1932) and *The Three Musketeers* (1933), only occasionally landing a bit role in a big-budgeted feature at a major studio.

In Conflict *(1936)*

It was his old mentor John Ford who gave Wayne the opportunity to progress from a highly acceptable action-film lead into a major screen name. The studio was United Artists; the film was *Stagecoach* (1939). To flesh out his cast of seasoned but not bigname players (Claire Trevor, Thomas Mitchell, and John Carradine), Ford secured Wayne to portray the Ringo Kid. This classic picture found him saving the coach passengers from an Indian attack, romancing Trevor, and shooting it out with Tom Tyler and his gang. Wayne gave an added dimension to his characterization, and his career received a permanently prosperous rebirth.

A flow of brawny screen roles followed, making Wayne a top box-office fixture. They included Ford's *The Long Voyage Home* (1940), a Eugene O'Neill tale of men at sea; De Mille's period epic *Reap the Wild Wind* (1942); and a 1942 remake of *The Spoilers* with Marlene Dietrich and Randolph Scott. In the years following his *Stagecoach* triumph, Wayne made screen love to such celebrated leading ladies as Joan Crawford, Paulette Goddard, and Susan Hayward.

A football injury and his age kept Wayne out of World War II combat, but he played war heroes in such films as *Flying Tigers* (1942), *The Fighting Seabees* (1944), and Ford's ode to the navy, *They Were Expendable* (1945).

In the postwar years, there seemed to be no stopping Wayne's ever-increasing popularity. The vehicles were certainly adequate—*Fort Apache* (1948), *Red River* (1948), and *Three Godfathers* (1948) were top westerns, while *Sands of Iwo Jima* (1949) was an outstanding war movie. For this last feature, John was nominated for an Oscar, but he was beat out by Broderick Crawford for *All the King's Men*.

By this time, Wayne was a steady member of the top ten box-

With Maureen O'Hara in The Quiet Man *(1952)*

office draws. His strong force camouflaged behind a soft-spoken voice, an animal magnetism overshadowed by a respect for "good" women, and a fierce ruthlessness in fighting for the right cause—all were irresistible qualities to moviegoers despite the jibes of the usually disenchanted critics. "Nobody likes my pictures but the public," Wayne has stated over the years. There have been some exceptions. John Ford, who saw Wayne as his favorite leading man, cast him in such worthy efforts as *The Quiet Man* (1952). Shot in Ireland and filled with Gaelic charm, this film presented Wayne opposite his favorite leading lady, Maureen O'Hara.

In 1960, Wayne made his directing debut in *The Alamo,* in which he also starred as Davy Crockett. Despite a commercially oriented cast, the result was a 199-minute bore.

With his waistline bulging and his face creasing, Wayne lumbered through the sixties in features like *The Sons of Katie Elder* (1965), *War Wagon* (1967), and *El Dorado* (1967). There was also a 1964 bout with cancer that he admirably surmounted. In 1969, he at long last won an Oscar, for his role in *True Grit* as Rooster Cogburn, the one-eyed U.S. marshal. As he collected his trophy, Wayne jokingly told the audience, "If I'd known, I'd have put the eye patch on thirty-five years earlier."

Wayne's annual output of features goes on. Besides his frequent westerns, there have been some police capers, such as *McQ* (1974) and *Brannigan* (1975), the latter filmed in London. Certainly the casting coup of the decade occurred when it was announced that Duke and Katharine Hepburn would join forces for *Rooster Cogburn* (1975), a sequel to *True Grit.*

And so John Wayne, celluloid's big living legend (recently separated from his third wife Pilar), continues onward. As a star whose pictures have grossed over $400 million, he explains, "I've been around movies long enough for millions of people to have been born, have kids, and die. But I'm still working."

Films

1927: The Drop Kick. *1928:* Mother Machree, Hangman's House. *1929:* Salute, Words and Music. *1930:* Men without Women, Rough Romance, Cheer Up and Smile, The Big Trail. *1931:* Girls Demand Excitement, Three Girls Lost, Men are Like That (a.k.a. Arizona), Range Feud, Maker of Men. *1932:* Haunted Gold, Shadow of the Eagle (serial), Hurricane Express (serial), Texas Cyclone, Lady and Gent, Two-Fisted Law, Ride Him Cowboy, The Big Stampede. *1933:* The Telegraph Trail, Central Airport, His Private Secretary, Somewhere in Sonora, Life of Jimmy Dolan, The Three Musketeers (serial), College Coach, Baby Face, The Man from Monterey, Riders of Destiny, Sagebrush Trail. *1934:* Lucky Texan, West of the Divide, Blue Steel, The Man from Utah, Randy Rides Alone, The Star Packer, The Trail Beyond, 'Neath Arizona Skies. *1935:* Lawless Frontier, Texas Terror, Rainbow Valley, Paradise Canyon, The Dawn Rider, Westward Ho! Desert Trail, New Frontier, Lawless Ranger. *1936:* The Lawless Nineties, King of the Pecos, The Oregon Trail, Winds of the Wasteland, The Sea Spoilers, The Lonely Trail, Conflict. *1937:* California Straight Ahead, I Cover the War, Idol of the Crowds, Adventure's End. *1938:* Born to the West, Pals of the Saddle, Overland Stage Raiders, Santa Fe Stampede, Red River Range. *1939:* Stagecoach, The Night Riders, Three Texas Steers, Wyoming Outlaw, New Frontier, Allegheny Uprising. *1940:* Dark Command, Three Faces West (a.k.a. The Refugee), The Long Voyage Home, Seven Sinners. *1941:* A Man Betrayed (a.k.a. Wheel of Fortune), Lady from Louisiana, The Shepherd of the Hills, Lady for a Night. *1942:* Reap the Wild Wind, The Spoilers, In Old California, Flying Tigers, Reunion in France, Pittsburgh. *1943:* Lady Takes a Chance (a.k.a. The Cowboy and the Girl), In Old Oklahoma (a.k.a. War of the Wildcats). *1944:* The Fighting Seabees, Tall in the Saddle. *1945:* Flame of the Barbary Coast, Back to Bataan, Dakota, They Were Expendable. *1946:* Without Reservations. *1947:* Angel and the Badman, Tycoon. *1948:* Fort Apache, Red River, Three Godfathers, Wake of the Red Witch. *1949:* She Wore a Yellow Ribbon, The Fighting Kentuckian, Sands of Iwo Jima. *1950:* Rio Grande. *1951:* Operation Pacific, Flying Leathernecks. *1952:* The Quiet Man, Big Jim McLain. *1953:* Trouble along the Way, Island in the Sky, Hondo. *1954:* The High and the Mighty. *1955:* The Sea Chase, Blood Alley. *1956:* The Conqueror, The Searchers. *1957:* The Wings of Eagles, Jet Pilot, Legend of the Lost. *1958:* I Married a Woman, The Barbarian and the Geisha. *1959:* Rio Bravo. *1960:* The Alamo (also director), North to Alaska. *1961:* The Comancheros. *1962:* The Man Who Shot Liberty Valance, Hatari, The Longest Day. *1963:* How the West Was Won, Donovan's Reef, McLintock!

1964: Circus World. *1965:* The Greatest Story Ever Told, In Harm's Way, The Sons of Katie Elder. *1966:* Cast a Giant Shadow. *1967:* War Wagon, El Dorado. *1968:* The Green Berets (also codirector), Hellfighters. *1969:* True Grit, The Undefeated. *1970:* Chisum, Rio Lobo. *1971:* Big Jake. *1972:* The Cowboys. *1973:* The Train Robbers; Cahill, U.S. Marshal. *1974:* McQ. *1975:* Brannigan, Rooster Cogburn.